Miss Lynn

My Delusional Mother

by
Andy Accioli

This book is a work of non-fiction. Some names have been changed. All of the letters written by Miss Lynn included in this book are printed exactly as she wrote them without spelling, grammar or punctuation corrections.

I write under the pen name of Andy Accioli. My birth name is Andrew Acciaioli.

Miss Lynn: My Delusional Mother
Copyright © 2014 Andy Accioli

The author's website: http://www.AndyAccioli.com

Published by: DamoraBooks.com

ISBN: 978-1507623930

Dedication

This book is dedicated to Kathy, my wife of over 35 years as well as our grown children: Kristen, Matthew, Michael and Mark who have supported me in all of my endeavors and especially for having personally endured Miss Lynn.

Acknowledgements

A special thanks to Diane Caputo my tireless and skilled editor who strove relentlessly – and I MEAN relentlessly - to get this book to be the best from its first rough draft months ago right through its publication.

Joy Bianco thanks for reviewing my book and providing me with feedback.

I also appreciate the additional stories provided by Elizabeth "Liz" Ricci, Jeanne Page, Angela & Jack Cimino, Carol & Zee Santos, Maryann Savastano and Marie Payne.

Finally, I wish to pay tribute to two of my favorites who are no longer with us:

Maureen Hassett although you have passed, you were like a big sister to me and stood by me during stressful times in dealing with Mom and her shenanigans.

Uncle Ernie (Savastano), although you too have passed, during the years of your being a tour escort for my company, Hartley Tours, you gave me my share of *agita* (sending me to a drag bar under a false pretense…leading my senior citizen passengers on an Easter egg hunt along a major highway…diverting one of my tour buses to look for Frank Sinatra's birthplace…). The pranks that you pulled being a member of *The Kids* have continued to keep me laughing over the years.

Table of Contents

Introduction

Meet my mom, Evelyn Savastano Acciaioli, who would eventually become known as Lynn Simmons after several marriages.

1950 was steeped in family tradition: households had a mom and a dad. Dads went out to work each day while moms remained home, tended to their children and maintained an immaculate household; being sure all dirty laundry was scrubbed clean daily – usually by hand – and hot meals were prepared from scratch morning, noon and night.

Although these well defined roles for men and women, particularly in the Italian culture, may have worked for men and women over the centuries, Mom sought a life and career far from the washboard.

Dad gave her an ultimatum, surely egged on by his *familia*: stay home where women belong and be a good wife and mother…or else. Mom accepted Dad's "or else" challenge. They divorced and she set out to show Big Andrew, my dad, and *the other end*, his family, that they were stuck in the past with their closed minds as she began her journey to have a career despite having a five year old child, me.

Mom would not have to think outside the box as she refused to be boxed in. This game of life came with rules, rules which were never meant to apply to her.

Whether in her career(s), her life or her relationships, reality – past or present – was what she said it was regardless of what actually, factually transpired. An example of this would be during her later years, when she insisted she only visited the gambling casino close to her home only twice since it opened a number of years ago. The reality was she was there at least once, sometimes two or three times a week, as proven by her ATM cash withdrawals recorded on her bank statements and her image captured by casino security cameras. When confronted she maintained her position, *her reality,* of having frequented the casino only two times since it opened and threatened to sue anyone who said otherwise.

Mom deluded herself, and others, with her portrayal as a savvy travel business owner when in reality her business was on the verge of ruin, forcing me to step in and take over her successfully bankrupt enterprise and turn it around before returning it to her with a clean balance sheet so she could destroy it again. And again.

After three marriages and a series of men in our home, one would think she would have a handle on relationships. Far from it. Sad to say her true love, her soul mate, her one-and-only was a fictional character called David who was simultaneously a wealthy Wall Streeter, a heart surgeon, a lawyer and a commander of an aircraft carrier during the Gulf War. Most children eventually leave their imaginary friends behind, but Mom's David remained as real to her when she was dying as the day she first encountered (invented) him in New York City over fifty years ago while attending training classes to sell hair coloring products.

Whether at home as a youth, away at school, or during my thirty-five year marriage, Mom would periodically author groundless hate letters filled with spite, which always expressed her current mood and responded to her perception of what had happened rather than what actually occurred. I, along with most everyone else, was out to undermine Miss Lynn. It was all a conspiracy and she spent her life trying to get to the bottom of it.

Her actions and words either in the form of vilifying letters lacking an iota of truth (some included in this book) or nasty telephone conversations would drive people away. Yet after they would no longer bother with her, she would wonder where they went.

This was the case with my four children, her grandchildren. The way Mom treated my wife and me as they were growing up eventually caused them to not want to have anything to do with their nana from their late teens through their early adulthood.

The only two people who would remain with Miss Lynn during her topsy-turvy life and ultimately be by her deathbed while she agonized in a semi-conscious state for days? Kathy, my wife, and I.

1. At the Cuzzoni's

In 1950 an apartment complex here in Rhode Island would be considered a triple decker tenement house. When responding to a question as to where you lived, your answer would not be a street address but the name of the person who owned the house where your apartment was located. After Mom and Dad married they lived at the Cuzzoni's, which was located on Silver Spring Street in Providence, a couple of miles from where they were both born and raised.

While at the neighborhood "baby doctor", pregnant Mom met pregnant Liz in the waiting room. As living in Rhode Island would have it, Liz and her husband happened to live diagonally across the street from the Cuzzoni's. Mom quickly took charge of the relationship. In Mom's estimation, Liz should be driven to the hospital immediately, and she offered to call my dad to drive her to Women and Infants Hospital. When Liz said her baby doctor, Dr. Zinno, told her it would be a week or two before she would deliver, my mother responded, "What do these doctors know?"

A week later, Liz delivered her daughter, Jeanne. I followed three days later. Mom and Liz became lifelong friends as a result of that chance meeting and the subsequent overlapping hospital stays. Jeanne and I have also enjoyed a 63 year friendship, oftentimes commiserating about our mothers. I assume our moms had similar conversations about us.

Two weeks after I was home, Mom convinced Liz to put us in strollers and take me to meet my Grandmother Savastano, a two mile brisk fall walk in each direction. As a result of this lengthy excursion, Liz ended up back in the hospital hemorrhaging.

A few weeks after this, Mom and Liz were chatting when Mom confided to Liz she had already started me on Pablum. Liz said Dr. Zinno instructed her not to give Jeanne Pablum so soon. Mom responded, "He told me the same thing, I defied him and started giving it to Rusty in his formula." Hence my weight problem lasting all my life. Ah, 'Rusty'...*don't ask.* Mom continued, "And I've already started potty training him. All I do is hold him on the potty seat until he goes." Hence my rushing to the bathroom at the slightest urge to purge.

It was not long before a first floor apartment became available right next to the Acciaioli compound on Langdon Street. Zero options on this one. The Acciaioli's would leave the Cuzzoni's and join the Acciaioli compound, sort of.

I could roll in any direction and find a cousin. Life was simple, life was good.

Not that I have any direct memory of when I was three but pictures show we had a wedding for my cousin Mary in our yard. She was the daughter of my mother's sister, Nella, whose husband, Joe, refused to give permission for his daughter to marry. Enter Auntie Evelyn, my mom, to break the longstanding Italian tradition of parental marriage consent or no marriage. She provided a wedding reception venue for Mary: our backyard.

This was the first memory of my parents fighting: Dad supporting the fatherly right to approve who would marry his daughter and Mom not allowing a custom to get in the way of throwing a wedding bash for her niece and the man she loved.

According to Mom during the years following my birth, she attempted to be the perfect wife and mom. Yet she wanted more.

It turned out the *more* was a sales job with the local Ironrite ironing machine dealer.

2. Lights, camera, pillowcase.

In the late 40's and early 50's a new ironing appliance found its way into a number of American homes. Housed in a large metal box, about the size of two computer desks pushed together, was a machine that would free up happy homemakers from the arduous task of standing at an ironing board, pushing and pulling a heavy, heated iron: the Ironrite Ironer.

The Ironrite had a large muslin covered roller which would press against an equally large heated metal surface; rotating and pulling the item to be ironed. Your hands were free to position what had to be ironed as the roller was controlled by your knees: right knee against the lever would cause the roller to clamp against the heated iron tray and activate the roller, left knee against the left lever would pause the roller, ridding those pesky creases with extra heated pressure.

The Ironrite Ironer Company based in Mount Clemens, Michigan established a local dealer network to distribute its innovative ironing apparatus to eager housewives across the nation. Among them was Evelyn Acciaioli.

I was four when our Ironrite invaded most of the space in our tiny living room. As any curious young child would, I nagged my mother into letting me give it a spin. She instructed me to never place my tiny fingers near the roller before allowing me to iron a flat piece such as a pillowcase or dish towel. Who irons pillowcases or dish towels? Obviously happy housewives in 1954 finding housework pleasurable and ironing therapeutic.

One pillowcase and I was hooked. Other kids would beg to go out and play, I would beg to iron.

The Ironrite's roller was not the only wheel turning. The wheels started to twist in Evelyn's imagination. Having seen live, local television commercials for the Ironrite, she thought it would be a novel idea to use me on TV demonstrating how uncomplicated this ironing machine really was: even a four year old could use it.

After contacting the local Ironrite dealer, she pitched the idea of having her son demonstrate how easy it was to use an Ironrite on television. They agreed to this novel sales approach.

In those days all local commercials were done live in the studio; your set was alongside the set where the newscasters sat. Relying on my memory of 59 years ago, I believe Art Lake delivered the news while Bunny North was assigned to be the weather "girl" on WJAR's newscasts. Once Art said "We'll be right back after a commercial message from Ironrite", the lights went dark on Art and Bunny and came up on Mom and me.

How did Mom get in MY act? Apparently she negotiated the deal to be included.

Later in life when I pressed Mom for the details of my television stardom, she recalled saying something like: "Hello, ladies, I'm Lynn Wright and this is my four year old son, Andrew. We're here to show you how quick and easy it is to make ironing less of a chore. With the Ironrite Ironer, you can sit and relax while you feed all of your wrinkled clothes and flat cloth items through our revolutionary roller system. Andrew will now show you how he can iron a wrinkled pillowcase." *Lynn holds up a wrinkled pillowcase to the camera. I iron the pillowcase. Lynn holds up the wrinkle-free pillowcase to the camera.* "Wrinkles are gone in seconds with the Ironrite. So simple, my four year old son can use it." Mom said I added (while the camera was still rolling): "I iron shirts, my dad's pants, sheets…"

Lights out on us. Lights came up on a chuckling Art and Bunny. Art remarked, "Quite a worker you have." Lynn Wright called back from the darkened set: "I only let him iron a pillowcase every now and then."There you have it. A star was born. Not me. The star, or at least she thought, was Lynn Wright.

Adios Evelyn Savastano Acciaioli. Hola Lynn Wright.

We celebrated our celebrity by walking from the WJAR-TV studio, located on an upper floor of the Outlet Department Store in downtown Providence to the nearby Woolworth's lunch counter overseen by my mom's sister-in-law, my Auntie Tina. I probably ordered my favorite: mashed potatoes with gravy. Instead of a small side dish, my aunt would use a large plate to plop a mountain of potatoes covered by what seemed like a bucket of brown gravy.

Lynn Wright probably had a coffee and cigarette while anxiously waiting for someone from TV-land to discover her at the Providence, Rhode Island Woolworth's counter as a result of her new fame: The Ironrite girl.

As for me, being a one commercial wonder was okay. A four year old has much bigger things to be concerned about: can we go home so I can play with my cousins and friends?

We arrived home greeted by my seething father. Not sure which triggered his anger more: His wife leaving the house as Evelyn Acciaioli and returning as Lynn Wright, or having his "women should stay at home" thinking violated by a wife not only working, but on public display and seen by viewers across the entire state.

Who would have thought a mother would use her four year old to not only sell more Ironrites, but to launch her own television persona?

It would appear Mom's career goals were at odds with my dad's – and his family's – vision of what a typical Italian wife's role should be in their *familia*.

According to Mom, confirmed by my dad, we would go to various family events and I would play with my cousins while Mom and Dad would go their separate ways. The only other time they would be reunited was when we would leave. Occasionally Mom was AWOL, out demonstrating the ironer or appearing as The Ironrite Girl somewhere. As though my father was not already fuming and furious enough over his wife's absence from his side (or at least arriving with him), his mother would stoke the flames by wondering aloud who wore the *pantaloni* in our family: him or my mother.

In those days families would live close to each other as though they were living in a Godfather type compound. Replacing the secured fenced perimeter and fortified gates would be an old Italian woman, wooden spoon in hand, more vicious than any pit bull ever created if you harmed her young. The price Italian mamas would expect to extract from their children in return was not much: only absolute control over every facet of their lives.

My Grandmother Maggie Acciaioli was no exception. According to my mother, Grandma - along with Dad's family - was the cause of their constant bickering: His family wanted to control our family and my dad lacked the cojones to tell them to stick their wooden spoons where the sun did not shine.

Dad argued this had nothing to do with his family but everything to do with ours and mom not being a *normal*, stay-at-home wife and mother.

Within a year, Mr. Acciaioli and Ms. Wright separated and raced to divorce court.

3. Divorce

Getting a divorce in 1955 was rare. An Italian-Catholic getting a divorce during this time period was rarer still. There were mainly two reasons for a judge to grant a divorce: A cheating spouse or a mentally or physically abusive spouse. Of course, most married plaintiffs seeking to divorce would select the highly subjective mental spousal abuse option not easily disproved by the defending spouse.

Contrary to the urging of both my mom's and dad's families to remain married in spite of their constant quarreling, my mom chose the mental abuse argument and was granted the divorce. They would share child custody: Weekdays I would remain with my mother, weekends with my dad.

Evelyn walked out of court 29 years old with a son, divorced and broke, but with her independent spirit intact. Our future looked precarious at best.

During the beginning of the divorce, we lived with Mom's sister, Pearl, her husband, Sammy, and their son, Ernie. Auntie Pearl was a pint-sized woman who would spend her days cleaning and cooking. Since Mom worked both a full-time and part-time job, most of my time was spent with my aunt. Whenever she would cook – which in an Italian household would be all the time – I would sit on top of a nearby step stool as both of us chatted away.

Mom would sleep on their living room couch while I slept with my cousin Ernie, who was twelve years older than me. Each school morning, like clockwork, Auntie Pearl would come into our room and yell at Ernie to get up for school. Every morning Ernie would tell her to leave him alone, he wanted to sleep. And every morning this tiny Italian lady would morph into Ninja Mom, finally entering the room with a broom and whacking my cousin the way you would an area rug on a clothes line. Eventually he'd get the message, dress and head off to school.

After a few months, Mom managed to save enough money for us to live on our own in a second floor attic apartment only a mile away from my dad, who had returned to live with his family.

As I recall, our Malvern Street apartment came furnished with the exception of a refrigerator, which was something Mom could not afford at the time. Since it was winter, she would put food requiring refrigeration in a metal box out on the roof covering the outside entrance within reach of our pantry window. That winter included some mild days, which resulted in spoiled food, which resulted in both of us being diagnosed by our family doctor with food poisoning.

Weekends Mom would drive me to my Acciaioli grandparents' house to spend time with my dad. In retrospect, remembering the close proximity of our living arrangements, I believe it was a result of Mom not wanting to move too far away from my dad, hoping they might reconcile, and my dad moving back in with his family for the same reason.

Of course, in the traditional Italian neighborhood they inhabited, family, friends and neighbors would be watching carefully to see what the newly divorced man was going to do: Would he move back in with his family, or into his own apartment? If he chose the apartment, tongues would immediately start wagging that it was scandalous, a gigolo-type thing to do, and proof positive he was the guilty party in the divorce due to all his philandering.

One time when Mom picked me up to return to our home, she reminded my dad that he had not paid his ten dollar weekly child support (worth around $86 today) which was due on the previous Friday. After all these years, this memory lingers within me: He took out a ten dollar bill and said something to the effect of, you want the ten dollars, here is your ten dollars, before throwing the bill on the ground. Mom got out of the car and retrieved the money; quite frankly we desperately needed it. After picking up the ten dollar bill, she waved to my dad's family, who were gathered in front of the living room windows to enjoy the show.

Regardless of what my mom would do in her life, to me or my family, I would always think back to how she was humbled and humiliated by my dad, forced to pick money up out of the dirt while his family watched.

Thanksgiving dinner was with Mom's family at Nonne's (grandmother's) house the first year after the divorce. Because our car was on the fritz, we had to take three buses to get to my grandmother's. While we were walking from the bus stop, we stopped at a fruit stand so Mom could buy various pieces of fruit to fill a wicker cornucopia basket we were bringing to my grandmother's Thanksgiving meal. Thinking back, the fruit cost

Mom just over a dollar, which left us with change from the two dollars we had left after the bus passes were purchased to get us there and home.

Arriving at Nonne's house we were greeted by other family members. Time passed and no move was made to serve dinner. It appeared as though they were waiting for us to leave before they began their Thanksgiving feast. Break bread with a divorcee and her kid? Not under Nonne's roof. Not receiving an invitation to stay, we left.

While waiting for the bus, I asked Mom where we were going to have Thanksgiving. She said we were going home and she would cook our dinner. Shortly after arriving back at our apartment we sat down for our holiday meal of scrambled eggs and toast. While eating, Mom vowed this would be the only time we would not have turkey for our Thanksgiving dinner; she would make sure the future would be better for us.

One night while Mom was working her second job, a part-time position, my babysitter and I were startled by loud footsteps coming up our stairs followed by even louder banging on our door. She quietly rushed me into the bedroom and told me to stay in there with the door closed, everything would be all right. I heard a male voice say they were from the Providence Police Department to investigate Evelyn and her son. Carol, my babysitter, told them we were not at home. I peeked out of the bedroom door and did not recognize one man but the other one was Dad's electrician friend, Anthony. Providence Police Department? Even at that early age I knew Anthony was not a policeman. They left, and Carol allowed me to stay up and wait for my mom to come home so we both could tell her what happened.

When Mom arrived home, she was initially upset Carol had allowed me to stay up, but after Carol briefed her as to what had transpired, her concern over my lack of sleep turned into a fiery rage against "Big Andrew", my dad. The only thing I am able to recollect from that particular rant was the word *unfit*. My mom said something along the lines of my dad wanting to prove her unfit to raise a child.

The next time I would hear that word *unfit* was during a trip we took to Florida. Wait a minute, little money for food, vacation in Florida? What happened was one of my dad's cousins had married a woman named Pat from Florida. Pat and Dad's cousin divorced around the same time as Mom and Dad, and she moved back to Florida. The January following our Thanksgiving scrambled egg feast, Pat invited Mom and me to come down for a visit along with a mutual friend, Mary. Mary was a widow and single mom raising a son after the death of her husband. She also had a car and the wherewith all to make our trip possible.

Mary picked us up and drove us straight to Seekonk, Massachusetts, where we spent the day and night. Even though I was very young, I knew Florida was a long way off, why did we stop driving only minutes from home? I was annoyed and wanted to annoy my mom as well by asking questions. She explained we would be getting up during the night to depart for Florida.

Many years later when I asked her why in the world we headed east to Seekonk rather than south to Florida, she took credit for tricking anyone my dad might have covertly sent to spy on us and throwing them off the scent. I really cannot fault her for that, having experienced Dad's friend pretending to be a Providence cop hoping to catch her in the act with another man to prove she was *unfit* as a mother.

During the night, we loaded into Mary's car and were Florida bound.

The vacation was amazing. I never imagined we could leave snowy Rhode Island and a few days later be on a warm, sunny beach. We were not the only ones enjoying the sun and surf; my dad and his cousin, Pat's ex-husband, had also found their way to our beach. As naïve as a five year old could be, I was ecstatic Dad would be joining us on our Florida vacation.

As they approached us, both Mom and Pat started screaming at them, while Mary attempted to distract her son and me away from the budding brawl on the beach. My dad was waving a Brownie camera (popular at the time) around, using the word *unfit* before he and Pat's ex retreated and stormed off the beach. Mom was upset. Pat was upset. Even I was upset that my dad did not stay with us or even acknowledge the fact I was there.

Not long after we returned home, my mom had to go to court to retain custody of me in an action instituted by my dad over her being an *unfit* mother by transporting me out-of-state without first obtaining his written permission. Her claim was that she had obtained his oral approval. An obvious case of she said, he said. The family court sided with my mom.

On the surface it appeared as though my dad's love for me provoked his fevered attempts to take me away from Mom. Not so. As I look back over the years, he was acting not as a father worrying about the welfare of his only child, but more as a vengeful man who had been scorned and wanted to inflict the highest possible pain on his opponent, Mom, by branding her *unfit* and taking her son away. Had he been successful, his street cred with his *familia* would have increased exponentially.

I am pretty sure that influencing this domestic espionage was the country-wide frenzy stirred up by Senator Joe McCarthy and his "We'll get them before they get us" era: A time when even the most mild mannered fancied themselves 007 wannabees, finding intrigue in the mundane with the only requirement being a Brownie camera.

4. On the Move

We lived in our small attic apartment on Malvern Street for about a year before Mom met Joe Stefano. He became the love of her life, and she told me – as well as everyone else – that she and Joe were married. Supposedly it was one of those quickie Las Vegas marriages, except I don't remember Mom being away at any time to go the route of Vegas "I do's". But if Mom claimed they were married, they were married. More or less.

The move to our home in Lincoln, RI immediately followed their "marriage" as our apartment was much too small for the three of us. Apparently here is where my mom's name unofficially *officially* changed from Evelyn to Lynn. (A throw back to her Ironrite commercial days?)

Joe operated a window replacement business, which meant that Lynn now operated a window replacement business in Pawtucket, RI. I used to go to their office with them on Saturdays. On many occasions I would observe Mom charming customers into buying replacement windows and doors. Joe and she would constantly argue, as she would promise the customers anything to get the sale, leaving Joe the difficult if not impossible job of fulfilling orders Lynn had underpriced or promised delivery without checking a tight delivery schedule.

One Saturday as we were rushing to the office from Lincoln, Mom was pulled over for speeding and ticketed. She told the policeman she was going to fight the ticket and she did.

Because we arrived at the court house early, Mom decided we had time to grab breakfast at a nearby coffee shop. As we were leaving, there was an emaciated hound dog sitting at the door looking in. Checking the dog for a tag revealed it had none. Mom returned to the coffee shop and bought the dog a donut, gave it to him, patted him on the head and we started to walk back to the courthouse. Sensing the pooch was following us, Mom turned and sure enough our new friend was right behind us. Since it was a frigid day and she had no idea how long the docket of cases would be, she led the dog to our car, cracked the door window open a little and put the pooch inside out of the cold.

The courtroom was packed with other traffic violators. As the judge called his first case, Mom jumped up and interrupted him. He looked at her, probably anticipating her using some sort of insanity plea for hijacking the proceedings. "Excuse me, your honor. Can you tell me how long this will take, because I have a cold and hungry dog I just rescued waiting outside in our car, and I don't want to leave him for too long." Incredibly, the judge waved her forward. I was not sure whether my mother would be sent to jail for butting in or not.

After a few minutes she came back to where I was sitting and motioned to me to go with her. As we left the courthouse she told me the judge was an animal lover too and dismissed her case. Getting back to the car and our tail wagging new friend, Mom decided to name him Lucky: Her good luck charm for getting her out of the speeding ticket court case. I guess Lucky was pretty lucky himself to have adopted us and now reside in his forever home.

One time while Carol was babysitting I was rummaging around in some boxes in our living room closet and found my mother's original birth certificate specifying she was born in 1928 and not 1931 as she would tell people when they would ask her age. This tidbit of information was a golden "Get Out of Chores" card to a seven year old who could not wait for his mom to return home from work. Sharing what I had discovered with Mom, she yelled that I had no business going through her personal belongings and she would never again be able to trust me. Oh, well, I still had 1928 locked in my memory vault. (Later in life she would claim that her year of birth was 1926 adding two years onto her age. Why? I assume it was to start collecting full social security benefits earlier than she deserved. One would think the Social Security Administration would have a verification system in place to prevent this type of thing. Then again she started collecting full benefits in 1991, decades before her death. Perhaps the requirements to file were less stringent then.)

At some sort of gathering of Joe's family during the summer, Joe's brother and my mom had a conversation relative to my schooling. He spoke about the private school he sent his children to, St. Dunstan's in Providence. Mom was convinced that I should transfer there. Come September, I was enrolled at St. Dunstan's. Not bad, my third school and I was only in the second grade.

I was not the only one starting a new school. Mom decided to make a career move from selling window and door replacements, envisioning herself as one day owning a beauty salon. In order to do this she would have to go to hairdressing school. After dropping me off at St. Dunstan's she would continue on to cosmetology school.

Thanksgiving was unlike the previous year. Although we once again feasted on scrambled eggs it was in a hotel restaurant for breakfast rather than last year's dinner. The hotel was in New York City, and after our early morning breakfast we took our position outside on the sidewalk in the front row to enjoy the Thanksgiving parade. Later that afternoon we partook in a traditional turkey dinner at the hotel. Mom made good on her last year's vow that we would enjoy a turkey dinner on Thanksgiving Day. And what could be more spectacular than being at Macy's Thanksgiving parade?

The Lynn and Joe Show's curtain started closing right after Christmas. By spring their divorce happened as secretly as did their marriage.

We moved into an apartment on top of an auto body shop (formerly a laundry where my grandmother worked) right next to my grandmother's house in Pawtucket. Attending the private St. Dunstan's School was now out of the question as Mom could not afford the tuition. I was transferred back to public school, Nathanael Greene Elementary School. Mom continued her training to become a beautician.

Transferring to Nathanael Greene and to Mrs. Summerscale's class was serendipitous: There was a girl in that class by the name of Jeanne Ricci. When I went home and told my mother, she raced to the phone to call information for a listing for "Adolf Ricci", Jeanne's dad. The operator not only gave her the telephone number but their address as well: Power Road, less than a mile from us. She called the number and her old friend Liz answered. After briefly reminiscing about the previous two years, they agreed to get together the next day. The lives of the Ricci's and Acciaioli's had intersected for the second time. Little did we all know that this would be the pattern until Mom's death, 56 years later.

Ever the schemer, Mom asked the proprietors of the beauty salon located across from our apartment to allow her to "do heads" in their beauty salon on certain nights of the week, evenly splitting the revenue derived from all the new patrons she would bring into their salon. In return, the salon agreed to fudge the number of hours

Mom worked there. In those days, upon graduation from beauty school you had to work under the supervision of a licensed hairdresser for a period of time. By finagling her hours, she would qualify to open her own salon much more quickly after state testing.

It was then Lenny, a carpenter by trade, entered our lives, when Mom decided to convert the back two rooms of our apartment into a beauty salon. Soon Lenny became more than a carpenter and would often dine with us and hang out with Mom long after I went to bed.

With her approaching graduation, in an effort to increase her clientele, Mom would work practically every night and all day Saturday leaving little time to be motherly. A sitter had to be hired, preferably one that could live with us. Enter Alice, straight out of nanny central casting: A *Mrs. Doubtfire* on steroids. Originally from England, the senior citizen immigrated to the United States as a young woman. Her accent was as strong as her daily afternoon gin spiked tea.

Although the construction of my mom's home beauty salon had long since been completed, Lenny lingered. Most evenings he and Alice, easily 30 years older than he, would enjoy watching television and drink cup-after-cup of their special (as in gin spiked) tea or coffee.

I would rat them out to my mom, and she would admonish me to stop making up stories.

"It's the truth," I would respond, "I see them pour liquor from a bottle into their coffee or tea. Alice gives Lenny money to go to Candy's Liquor Store, and he comes back with liquor bottles."

"Lenny would never do that. He'd tell me first. Why do you make up stories?" Okay, don't believe me.

One night my dad called and wasted little time asking me if I had ever seen my baby sitter drinking. (How he found this out to this day is beyond me. I know I never told him what I knew.) Mom would always listen in on my dad's calls by holding the phone so both of us could hear the conversation. As an eight year old, I truthfully told him I did see them adding liquor to their tea and coffee.

Mom went bonkers. She grabbed the phone from me and told Dad I was a liar, before slamming the phone back into its wall cradle. After slapping my face she raged at me to get out of her house. I left the apartment and sat on the lower step of the stairway to the second floor. A cascade of clothes began falling on me as Mom shrieked for me to get my clothes and get out. More and more clothes rained down the stairs as I sat crying, wondering where I should go.

Nora, one of mom's closest friends, was the first to arrive. She screamed at me as loud if not louder than Mom, telling me how bad I was to betray my own mother. Two other friends of Mom's were next to arrive expressing similar sentiments.

After sitting at the bottom of the cold, clothes-strewn stairway for about an hour, Nora called down for me to pick-up my clothes and put them back where they belonged. As I passed her in the upper hall with an armful of clothes she cautioned me to not talk to my mother as "She never wants to talk to you again."

In the apartment Mom's other two close friends and she were feverishly searching for liquor bottles either empty or full, as she feared my dad would be visiting us any second along with representatives from children's services. Surely they would later testify as to my mother's *unfitness* by leaving me to be cared for by a drunk.

An inebriated (plastered) Alice was sitting at the dining room table with a cup of unspiked black coffee in front of her. I guess they were attempting to sober her up before the authorities arrived.

After I got all of my clothes back up to my room in a large pile on my bed, I heard the women, who were now in the kitchen, say they had gotten all of the bottles. Bravely venturing out of my room, I told them to look at the bottom of the trash can. They removed the bag which caught the refuse and saw what appeared to be a trap door; underneath they found two bottles.

I then led them into the would-be beauty salon, stood on one sink's drop back chair, pushed a ceiling tile aside, and removed the bottle that was leaning on the metal grid supporting the drop ceiling. Other tiles were removed, other bottles found. The most clever hiding spot was the water tanks behind the toilets. Removing the tank's lid in both bathrooms uncovered submerged bottles. Not only a great place to stow liquor, but an excellent way to keep the liquor cool as well.

The ladies left with boxes of empty, semi-empty and full liquor bottles as Mom decided it was too risky for her to dispose of them in our trash. Besides with as many bottles as were found, it would easily take many weeks if she trashed a couple of bottles a week.

Mom had managed to build a substantial client base at the beauty salon where she now worked full time and evenings. In light of the liquor incident and Alice's admission that both she and Lenny were alcoholics, Mom decided it was time to be home on a full time basis and officially opened Lynn's Beauty Salon. Alice and Lenny were no longer a part of Lynn's world.

For the first time in many years, even pre-divorce from my Dad, Mom was now always home, kind of like a stay-at-home mom.

One day as a friend and I were walking home from school for lunch, we spotted a fire engine parked in front of our building. My friend hollered, "Look, Andy, there's a fire truck in front of your place!" I told him it was nothing. Probably meant lunch was ready. Mom was never even a decent cook. She had to have a fire extinguisher within reach of our gas stove at all times.

Monday and Tuesday Mom was free from doing heads and would use those days to shop or run errands. She contacted Liz one Sunday night and asked if I could have lunch with Jeanne at her house the following school day as Mom would not be home to make my lunch. Liz agreed and the next day I walked across Power Road from my new school, St. Maria Gorretti's Parochial School to have lunch at Jeanne's. Lunch was more like having dinner: hot food made from scratch.

When I returned home after school, Mom was outside our apartment spray painting some plastic violin wall hangings gold. I never did like those ridiculous violins when they were white; I surmised a different color would not move them into my like column. As I climbed the hallway stairs the pungent aroma of fresh paint grew stronger with each step I took. Walking into the newspaper lined dining room, I gasped. The ivory colored walls I left hours earlier were painted black. Ditto for the living room.

As I was standing there in shock, Mom entered with the pukey gold violins asking, "What do you think?"

It is doubtful she appreciated her twelve year old's response to her Morticia-like spontaneous spurt of creativity: "Will the dead bodies be arriving soon?" I asked.

Mike, Mom's latest beau, was in town only weekends since he worked for a record company in Chicago. I thought: Wait 'til Mike sees this funeral home motif on Friday.

When Mom and Mike first met he was the VP of Sales for a leading local television and appliance distributor. The offer to become the national sales director for a well-known record label was a career move he had to take. I have little doubt had Mom not immersed herself in her business, our home would be in Chicago, and I would be attending my sixth school in less than six years.

He would be the only man in my mom's life who would be unafraid to lock horns with her when he felt his view was the right one. Mike and I made quite a team, two males Mom could not control.

A year after Mike was with the record company, it was consolidated into a much larger label based in Los Angeles. Although he was offered a promotion to remain with the company in LA, he refused feeling that the weekly commute to Chicago was bad enough but shuttling to and from LAX was not even in the equation. In time, he reasoned, Lynn might relent and consent to move to the Chicago area, but never in a million years would she relocate to California.

He was right: Mom gave him the ultimatum of moving to the West Coast himself or staying on the East Coast with us.

Before he concluded his employment with the label, a huge appliance dealer in the Springfield, Massachusetts area contacted Mike about coming on board. After discussing it with Mom, they reached an agreement that we would move to the Springfield area with him.

Mom worked in the beauty salon of Steiger's Department Store in Springfield. We bought a house in Windsor, Connecticut (approximately 20 miles from Springfield), and I transferred schools once more to St. Michael's in Hartford. Our parish school, St. Gabriel's would not accept transfer students once the school year began. Not really acquainted with the area, Mom called schools she saw listed in the telephone directory. Driving me from Windsor to St. Michael's that first day, we both developed a case of the queasies: Me, because I would be starting my sixth school in seven years, she because of where St. Michael's was located...smack dab in the middle of a black neighborhood. As we parked in front of the school she told me I did not have to go here, we could go home and find another school, if I preferred. We met with the principal, who brought me up to the seventh grade classroom. As I walked in, I noticed that I was one of three white boys in a class of twenty-four.

I remained at St. Michael's, even though St. Gabriel's contacted Mom over the following summer and offered to transfer me there in September. I refused. St. Michael's was providing me with a whole new vision of life now made up of different ethnicities from diverse backgrounds, teaching me that all people are the same: Black, white, middle-class, poor. Transferring to St. Gabriel's felt like I'd be moving backwards.

My weekly weekend visits to Dad's grew less frequent. It seemed pointless to leave my friends, bus it from Hartford to Providence for a weekend with my dad, when he would be out on Friday and Saturday nights, and working in his diner/store all day Saturday and until noon on Sunday. Although Mom thought I should keep up the visits, I felt as though a weekly call would suffice.

The monotony of doing heads finally got to Mom, and she answered a newspaper ad to become a regional representative for an international hair coloring company. Her duties would be to cover all of the beauty salons in New England, with the exception of the Greater Boston market, and promote their relatively unknown hair coloring line. She was offered the position, and the next thing we knew, Mike and I were driving Mom to New York City to start her six weeks of training at their New York headquarters.

Once home and in the field, her days would encompass long drives and long hours. She loved the control she had over beauty salon owners and beauty products distributors. Oftentimes if a distributor refused her products, she had a simple strategy: Go after salons that bought from the distributor(s) and offer impossible to pass up deals on her line if they cut business ties with the distributor(s) who refused to carry her products. Every salon stolen from a recalcitrant distributor energized and motivated her to work even harder.

New England sales were going through the roof. Her supervisor, who oversaw most of the East Coast, met with her to extend his congratulations at being such a dynamic sales force. He also mentioned that corporate had received letters of complaint about her strategy from area distributors bellyaching that she took their salon business from them and gave it to another distributor who carried Mom's line. According to what Mom told Mike and me over dinner, her response to her supervisor was, "If anyone in upper management has a problem with the way I'm running New England, have them contact me. Be sure and mention that I have had offers from other hair coloring companies."

No further conversations were held over her sales tactic. However, I do recall another dust up occurring in Springfield. Jack, who ran a downtown health and beauty aids store, was selling pallet loads of her hair coloring directly to the public less expensively than the distributors themselves could buy directly from her company.

Mom was right in the middle of this battle. She made an arrangement for Jack's store to purchase massive quantities of her hair coloring products from a local co-operating distributor of hers, thereby qualifying the distributor for maximum product discounts. The distributor made very little profit on orders from this one store but once the order was submitted, the entire shipment would be shipped directly to the store. In addition, the distributor would be at the maximum volume discount level and able to sell the hair coloring products to other retailers and salons at a higher price and make even greater profits.

Rumblings started reaching Mom that her company's upper management was not pleased with her latest strategy. Their feeling: It was hurting their upscale image to have their product sold at a discounted price point. Instead of appearing in the main lobby of the company's U.S. headquarters beating her chest while chanting mea cupa, Mom expanded and replicated this exact same sales technique by linking other retail health and beauty aids stores to her other loyal distributors thereby qualifying them for top tier discounts and providing herself with a grand slam marketing model for moving truckloads of product. Her sales volume turned down the volume of corporate nagging. There was no further mention of her sales model.

If corporate thought distributors were squealing like stuck pigs, they should have heard the beauty schools that were unable to participate in area styling competitions – run by none other than Mom - because they would not purchase Mom's hair coloring for their schools. Her strategy to crack into the beauty school market was to only allow student stylists from schools stocking her hair coloring products to compete.

To further punish those schools that did not stock her products, she had a whole lot of pain coming their way: She placed newspaper ads to encourage those considering going to a beauty school to attend her hair styling shows for free. Of course, Mom would permit *her* schools, those using her company's products, to set up tables to encourage students to enroll in their school. It was not long before non-participating schools of cosmetology saw things Mom's way. You have heard of The Godfather; Mom might have been called The Hair Color Godmother, along with other labels too crass to mention.

The point being, no one was going to stop her from getting her products into salons or into the hands of hairdressing students or on the shelves of health and beauty aid stores. No one. It was either her way or *her way*.

With all these hair styling shows came another unofficial *official* name change from Lynn to Miss Lynn. It almost sounded as though one should kneel and kiss a bottle of her hair coloring.

She would introduce herself as Miss Lynn for decades to come even when she moved on from the beauty business into travel.

Weekend visits to Dad, though infrequent now turned excruciatingly unbearable. With Mike returning to Rhode Island to head an appliance distributorship, I would no longer be able to enjoy the solitude of the bus ride; instead Mom would drop me off at Dad's before continuing on to Mike's place in East Providence. On the hour and a half drive to Providence I would be briefed about what to say to Dad and which questions I should ask to gather information for her. During the return trip to Connecticut I was debriefed as she sought the answers to her questions and any other morsels of Acciaioli gossip I happened to hear. After a few of these drives I learned how to coyly play her game and would talk about anything but the answers she sought to her questions.

Then I wised up and began answering her questions like any wisenheimer young teenager: If you want to know if Dad says anything about you, I suggest you ask him. After the expected five or ten minute tirade of how I was the most ungrateful son ever, the rest of the ride home would pass in total silence occasionally broken by Mom's attempts to sing along with Patsy Cline or whoever she happened to be listening to on one of the local country western stations. I would stare out my side window thinking, we're in the Northeast not in Tumbleweed, Wyoming. Mom's duet of "Your Cheatin' Heart" with Hank Williams doesn't cut it.

Once I did toss out a hot news item from *the other end*. The item: Dad and longtime girlfriend Val were getting married in June. Mom slammed on the brakes - thankfully no one was driving in back of us - and pulled the car over to the break down lane demanding all of the details. My game plan of "If you want the details ask Dad," didn't work this time as she refused to move the car unless I told her everything I knew. After sharing the little info I was told, our journey continued with her spewing venom of how despicable my dad was and how Val had some nerve marrying her husband. I silently thought: Your husband? What about Joe, Lenny, all the other guys and now Mike? As far as I knew besides Mom, Val was the only woman ever in my dad's life.

Years later I found out that Mom was sending postcards to Val, who was the executive secretary to the general manager of the Narragansett Beer Brewery, at her office (obviously passing through the mailroom and the hands of others en route to her desk) with all sorts of accusations about how she stole Mom's husband. Other cards accused Val of carrying on an affair with Dad while he and Mom were married. When my father spoke of these postcards, I asked to see them, still finding it difficult to believe that even Mom could be so vindictive, because I didn't want to admit that my mother could do such a thing. Val didn't want me to see them, I knew she wanted to spare me, but I insisted and she finally showed them to me. I was horrified by the sheer nastiness and malice, the falsehoods Mom had sent in postcard form to besmirch Val's personal and professional reputations. You marry my ex-husband, I'll show you...

During the early spring of my eighth grade year at St. Michael's, after dinner one evening Mom asked me which area high school I was considering. With Mom it was much better to make a direct statement rather than take a circuitous route: "Mom, I want to go into a junior (high school) seminary to become a priest." After a lengthy pause giving her ample time to tear up, she asked which one was in the area. I explained that I wanted to become a priest in the Carmelite Order and their junior seminary was located in Middletown, MA approximately 100 miles away.

I could feel her sense of loneliness creeping into the kitchen. Not only had Mike abandoned her by moving back to Rhode Island, but now her son would be 100 miles away from her, deserting her, as she put it.

Our split level house was sold within a matter of weeks, because it was located at the end of a secluded cul de sac which saw very few cars. Mom and Mike's relationship was falling apart. When the moving van came for our furniture, I realized the Miss Lynn and Mike Show was over: The furniture was headed for storage in Hartford rather than a home in Rhode Island.

With my graduation over, our furniture gone, new folks occupying our house, it was time to move on to our annual summer pilgrimage to New Hampshire and Maine. Nine or ten weeks of vacation for me, daily sales calls for Mom; after all, Northern New England ladies needed their God-given hair to be brought back to its *God-given* color too. Mom imported my RI cousins every week or two so I wouldn't be lonely.

During one stay in Hampton Beach, New Hampshire, Mom received a call from Adele, the representative with my mom's company handling the Greater Boston area. She was screaming into the phone about having just opened her mail to find her quarterly bonus check in the amount of a hundred thousand dollars. Mom had also received her bonus check for twelve thousand dollars.

Feeling as though something was wrong, she gave me the phone. I asked Adele to describe the check amount number. Her response, "One-zero-zero, zero-zero-zero." Sounded like a hundred grand to me. After handing the phone back to Mom who was still in a state of disbelief, she told Adele she would meet her half-way the next morning to verify the check amount.

Although it was after nine and we were an hour's drive away, Adele insisted on coming to us immediately. Mom agreed.

Zero to psychotic in one telephone call. Mom was incensed that Adele had received a bonus nearly ten times hers. Plus Adele's territory was a single city whereas Mom busted her butt covering six states. Who do they think they are? She was the one who put them on the map in New England, not Adele. "I'll fix them" she said, "I'm calling Jack [Springfield health and beauty aids Jack] to set up a meeting and tell him to cancel all his orders now on the books. And I'm calling my boss. He begged me to take over this goddamn New England position." And so on.

I tried to get her to cool down, but my words added more kerosene to her raging fire. She picked up the phone and said she was going to let her boss "have it". Not a good idea, I told her, at least not until she verifies Adele's check. Mom could not be stopped. Despite the late hour, she called him. Thank God his wife answered and told Mom he had not returned home yet. Mom explained it was an emergency that he calls her back; the Mrs. assured Mom she would have him return the call the moment he walked in their door.

She then proceeded to make a list of all the distributors she converted over to her hair coloring line, intending to call them in the morning to instruct them to lighten up on their orders. Mom expected to be rep'ing for one of her competitors and did not want them fully stocked with her present company's products.

Adele arrived bearing a box of Italian pastry from Boston's north end and the infamous check. She handed the envelope to Mom who removed the check, and I thought she was going to vomit. I took the check from her and noticed that it contained a faded dot after the first two zeroes. It was for one thousand dollars and even stated this in the line below the recipient's name as all checks do. Mom started to laugh with relief, Adele was devastated. "I spent every cent of the money in my head while driving up here. First thing tomorrow I was going to buy a new gold Cadillac."

Mom made coffee as we ate the pastry and had a good laugh. Adele mentioned that she even showed her mother, a little old rotund Italian lady, who lived on the first floor of their family house, and her mom agreed it was for *"Centomila Dollari"*. What was turning out to be a fun night was interrupted by the ringing phone. I looked at Mom, Mom looked at the phone, Adele looked at her cannoli.

Answering the phone, Mom told her boss to hang on and talk to someone special. She handed the phone to Adele, who proceeded to tell him her *Centomila Dollari* story which gave Mom time to concoct an emergency. Once the phone was handed back to her she began spinning her tale about needing a distributor sample kit immediately sent to her because she was calling on a large New Hampshire distributor and had run out of kits. Adele interrupted their conversation by telling Mom she had a couple of kits in the trunk of her car. Faux emergency resolved.

At the end of August we returned to Connecticut to hunt for an apartment for Mom. Since she was on the road extensively, a key consideration was proximity to the major highways passing through Hartford. It did not take long to determine East Hartford with all its newly constructed apartment complexes would be ideal.

Once Mom selected a perfectly located three room apartment the problem then became what to do with eight rooms of furniture from our former house which was in storage awaiting delivery. I don't recall what happened with the stored furnishings. I do know that Mom bought all new apartment-sized furniture. For the next week prior to leaving for school, my bedroom was the living room and my bed was an apartment–sized couch amidst floor to ceiling boxes of packed *essentials* from our old house.

The trip to deposit me at Our Lady of the Brown Scapular Junior Seminary in Middletown, MA was for the most part uneventful. Neither Hank Williams nor Patsy Kline was tuned-in to share our drive. Mom kept repeating that she would be all right. I'm not sure if that was meant to reassure me or her.

There was a brief freshman orientation when we arrived. Among other things, parents were told one Sunday of each month was set aside for parental visitation, where we could spend the day with them either on the school grounds or off. We kids were anxious to have our parents leave so we could unpack and get started with our new lives.

A couple of days later while I was in class, over the intercom I – and the entire school – heard, "Andrew Acciaioli please report to the office." On my way there I remember thinking; this has Miss

Lynn written all over it. The secretary told me that my mom was in the front parlor.

Opening the carved wooden door I was unsure of whether I should scream or burst out laughing. Mom stood there in a black dress, black stockings, black shoes and a black mantilla over her head. Too bad you failed to take it to the next level, Mom, and dye your hair black since you are in the hair coloring biz, but I was not bold enough to say that. Honestly, Mom looked like the Queen of Sorrows. The Queen of Sorrows roaring up in front of the seminary in her snazzy new gold Barracuda.

She said she was in the area so she thought she would stop by and see how I was doing and take back any dirty laundry. I said I guess I am doing the same as when you dropped me off on Sunday and over the past couple of days I've been here I really didn't have time to dirty up much laundry. Fortunately, for me, the bell rang and after a rushed good-bye I dashed to my next class to the jeers of my classmates, "Mommy had to come visit her little baby boy.

Grrrrrrrrr.

Over Thanksgiving break I informed Mom that I was not sure I wanted to become a priest and would probably be coming home for good after my January exams. She was elated. I'm not sure whether it was over my coming home or her being able to retire her black ensemble.

After exams, the racy Barracuda came up the seminary's driveway and it was time to say good-bye to my new friends. I had to move on. I mean, I'd had six school transfers during my elementary years. If I wanted to tie or break that record for high school, I had to step it up.

Mom had already submitted an application for a larger, two bedroom apartment located diagonally across the street from her present Burnside Avenue apartment. There was a construction related delay pushing the completion date to March instead of the scheduled January, meaning the living room by day would continue to be my bedroom at night.

East Hartford High School (EHHS) was a culture shock after so many years of Catholic school education. Being able to talk in class without chancing a nun calling Mom to scold her on her lack of parenting skills in rearing such an insolent child was heaven on earth.

One day during this period, we had an early dismissal just before noon. Not having moved to our larger apartment yet, I noticed my mom's car in her parking space. This was unusual as she should have been on the road a lot earlier than this. When I opened the door, I noticed her bedroom door opened and went in to find her in bed with the general contractor of the new apartment complex we were moving into. I'm guessing two bedroom apartments were hard to come by.

I aimlessly walked down Burnside Avenue to East Hartford center, not returning to the apartment until that evening.

As soon as I walked in, Mom attempted to explain what I *thought* I had seen. I would not discuss it with her, beyond my claim of knowing exactly what I saw, and told her to face reality, that this was not Kansas, Miss Lynn, and you do not have a dog named Toto. I had no desire to talk to her for days except for telling her I would be going to Rhode Island for the weekend. She offered to drive me. I declined: An hour and a half monolog attempting to recolor what I had witnessed? No thank you, a bus ride would be more palatable. A friend dropped me off at Hartford's bus station.

I had maintained telephone communication with Mike over the year since Mom and he called it quits. After calling and telling him I was coming to Rhode Island, he asked if I wanted to get together with him for lunch on Saturday.

At lunch we chatted about my transitioning into public school as well as my plans for the future after high school. He asked how Mom was doing. Not daring to tell him of her most recent hanky-panky as I secretly hoped for some future reconciliation between them, I told Mike she was doing fine adding, "But you know Mom."

Indeed he did know Mom, explaining how delusional she was, always imagining, "Everyone was out to get her: Her company, the neighbors, your dad, some of her family, even me. She never realized I only wanted what was best for her; she would always accuse me of outrageous lies. David, a New York heart surgeon she met while training for her job was waiting in the wings for her." He went on to say that after years of being with her he had finally had enough and decided to leave.

At the end of our lunch he did say he thought it best we not tell her of our meeting or our telephone calls. "Mike, one thing I'm not is suicidal." As we were leaving the restaurant he did tell me to stay in touch, and if Mom or I needed anything to give him a call.

My stomach knotted as the bus pulled alongside the Hartford bus/train station and I spotted the curbside gold Barracuda. After a rather cool greeting on my part, Mom immediately asked her usual post-trip debriefing question: "What did *the other end* have to say about me?"

Lacking any restraint, I responded: "Would you get it through your head, *the other end* couldn't care less whether you're dead or alive. They never ask about you, they never talk about you. Believe it or not, people have other things to talk about besides Miss Lynn."

During the brief ride back to the apartment and for the rest of that night, neither of us spoke, and that was just fine with me.

Most parents would want their children to study on a school night. Mom did too unless it was poker night at Martha and Joe's and they were down a player. Then Mom would be of the opinion that you can study when we get home, right now we need you to fill in. Teach 'em while they're young, right?

I loved Martha and Joe, who were born and educated in Czechoslovakia. Martha, a tall, beefy woman who was trained as a nurse ruled the roost. Joe, a slender, shorter-than-Martha man held a PhD in physics and was a professor at an area engineering college. Joe would laugh all the time and allow Martha free reign when it came to household matters, including the weekly poker sessions. Another neighboring couple would also play.

Mom developed a system to rile Martha over a non-poker issue either for our entertainment or to distract her from concentrating on the game. Oftentimes it dealt with how superior America was to their native Czechoslovakia.

A typical conversation during the game:
MOM: Martha, you have to admit, health care in America is superior to that in Czechoslovakia. I'll see your two and raise you two.

MARTHA: Here's mine two and two more I raise you. Vhat you tink, Czechoslovakia has best health care in vorld. I expert, a trained nurse.

MOM: Your two and I raise you two. Maybe you were a nurse over there but our standards are much higher.

JOE: I'm out. Martha, look at your cards.

MARTHA: Be quiet, Choe. Not easy like here to become nurse. Ve go to medical college. I raise you two more.

JOE: You can't raise any more, Martha. Pay attention.

MOM: I have three queens.

MARTHA: So many years ve train, ve can do surgery in emergency.

JOE: Nurses back home do not do surgery, Martha.

MARTHA: I no say ve did no surgery, I say ve trained to do surgery in emergency. Vhat you know, anyway, Choe?

JOE: *(shaking his head)* Look at your cards. Lynn has three queens.

MARTHA: Okay. Okay, I got the 10 of the spades, 3 of the diamonds…oh, okay, I out.

Honestly, it was worth getting home at midnight to start studying, they were such a hoot. And many times I would come home with my pockets filled with ill-gotten loot.

As a fifteen year old starting to feel a sense of independence, I sought another source of revenue to fund school related activities beyond Mom's Bank & Trust and birthday and Christmas gift money. Because I was not sixteen I had to obtain working papers from the school department in order to nab any part-timers' dream job: An usher at a single screen movie theater located in the middle of East Hartford center. If I worked a night shift, I would walk there after school and Mom would pick me up later that night when the theater closed.

Mom would usually arrive earlier than when my shift was over. When the manager, referred to as *Mr. Miserable* by the girls in the concession booth, saw her he would come out of his office and talk with Mom. One night after I had been there for a couple of weeks, Mom was not in the lobby when the theater was closing. *Mr. Miserable* said "Acciaioli, since I'm coming over to your place tonight, I told your mom she didn't have to bother coming to pick you up, I'll bring you." Whistles and bells. Whistles and bells. *Miserable's* coming to our place?

During the five minute drive to our townhouse apartment not a word was exchanged between *Miserable* and me. As I unlocked the front door with my *friend* in tow, I glared at Mom without saying a word and went down to my basement bedroom. Months before in order to avoid any activity that might be going on, I had relocated my room from the second floor bedrooms in our apartment to an unfinished room in the cellar.

Completing my homework, I was calling it a night right after hitting the bathroom. We only had one bathroom in the apartment and it was located near the bedrooms on the second floor. As I climbed the stairs, I heard THE noises coming from Mom's bedroom. When I passed her closed door en route back to the solace of my cave, I loudly remarked, "Get a hotel room."

The next morning, Mom was already in the kitchen before I surfaced from the basement, "I made lunch for you, honey." I did not respond.

"After *Mr. Miserable* left I was watching a loud television movie in my bedroom, I hope the noise didn't disturb you." Again, I did not say a word as I left the apartment and the lunch she made behind.

A friend of mine who was an after school shelf-stocker at Maxwell Drug Store one block down from *Mr. Miserable's* theater, told me Maxwell's was hiring. I walked there when classes were over, applied and was hired as a stock boy scheduled to start the following afternoon. Then I gleefully walked the next half-block and entered *Mr. Miserable's* office. Without a word I opened my backpack and dropped my crumpled usher's uniform shirt on his desk and walked out.

Mom was planning our summer jaunt to northern New England when I told her I wouldn't be going, that I didn't want to leave my job or my friends. Her compromise: I would be allowed to stay as long as a friend of hers moved in for the summer. I actually worked with her friend, Dottie, at Maxwell's. She was head of the cosmetics department and her sarcasm was classic. As I was stocking product across from Dottie's cosmetic counter, an older lady went up to her holding a tube of lipstick and asked, "Do you think this lipstick will make me look younger?" Dottie's caustic answer, "Your lips younger, the rest of your face not a chance."

Dottie moved in for the summer. Harry, Dottie's longtime older "special friend," would visit practically every night toting a 12-pack of Budweiser beer for his and Dottie's – mostly Dottie's – delicate palates. The beer came from Maxwell's, as Harry was the manager of the liquor department. Dottie would get more and more sarcastic toward Harry as the night went on; downing can after can of the brewski. And Harry just laughed with each put down.

Thankfully I would be out most times when Mom would call. This one night, Dottie was racing to Drunkland at a rapid clip when the phone rang and she answered the phone slurring her words and giggling. Mom, who was calling, demanded to speak to me. She asked if Dottie was drinking again because she gave her strict instructions: No drinking at our apartment. I told her Harry was over, we were finishing dinner and sitting around telling jokes. "What did you have for dinner?" snapped Mom. As I eyed the empty pizza box I said, 'Meatloaf, mashed potatoes with gravy, and green beans. Dottie's one heck of a cook."

All good things must come to an end and so did the summer, Dottie's *babysitting* gig and our frequent pizza, Chinese, McDonald's, Burger King, KFC dinners.

Once Mom returned she seemed re-energized and decided that since her distributor sales to beauty salons and schools continued to do well along with her growing retail business, she would concentrate her efforts on building retail sales. No longer chasing independent health and beauty aids stores, she would now chase pharmacy chains to stock her company's hair coloring line.

Arthur's Drug Stores operated pharmacies in the Hartford area. Although they comprised only three stores, they were sales powerhouses. Their ability to pump out loads of product from their pharmacies made shelf space extremely valuable, a fact they knew well and used to jawbone price concessions from all of their current suppliers, thereby making it practically impossible for a new vendor to get on their shelves. After a week of unreturned messages left for the buyer, Mom decided to pop in early one morning to their main store on Farmington Avenue.

As she later recounted her unannounced meeting to me, the buyer was there and she chewed him out for not having the courtesy to at least return her telephone calls. He asked her to show him what she had. She rebuffed his request. He asked her to dinner. He picked her up at 7 that night.

This turned into a weekly date. After about a month or so, Mom's hair coloring bottles occupied prime top shelve space at all Arthur's pharmacies. Only goes to show, if you can't sell 'em, date 'em.

Buyer guy was always friendly to me whenever he would pick Mom up. With the summer approaching he asked if I wanted a summer job working in one of their stores along with continuing my job at Maxwell's. Since I was now driving, commuting to any of their stores would not be a problem and since I was now driving, I certainly needed the extra money. I applied, and being an experienced stock boy, I was hired to work at their main store, frequently seeing *buyer guy*. I also saw *buyer guy's* wife and children: One my age, two younger.

When I told Mom that *buyer guy* was married with kids, I was amazed it didn't rattle her.

"We just go to dinner, it's business." I'll bet it is. And that business would be…

With my junior year of high school coming to an end my friend Alan told me his family was moving to Long Island and he would not be able to attend East Hartford High School for his senior year.

That night I asked Mom what she would do if her company demanded she relocate to New York right away in spite of this being my senior year at EHHS. "I'd tell them to go pound sand." Hmm. I would have to take a different approach, "Suppose you weren't in a position to tell them that and we had to make the move and I would have to miss out on spending my senior year with my high school friends." She responded as I knew she would by saying that we would seek out one of my friends' families, and I would reside with them in order for me to finish my last year at EHHS.

The next night, Alan and his family came over to discuss Alan staying with us for his senior year. He would spend the summer with his family at their new, Long Island home and return to our apartment Labor Day weekend.

As usual summer came and Miss Lynn was beautifying northern New England heads. This year I would not have to babysit Dottie and Harry. I had the apartment to myself.

Late one afternoon I stopped home from working at Arthur's during the day in order to shower and change into my Maxwell's uniform for my night shift. The doorbell rang. It was Father Paul from my father's family parish at St. Anne's in Providence.

I thought back to what one of my dad's single sisters had said about her encounter with Father Paul: After she gave her confession to him, he saw her outside the church and asked if she was busy. She said "Father Paul, I just went to confession in your confessional." He said "That was business, this is pleasure."

He asked if Mom was home. I told him no, she was away for the summer. "Well, when you talk to her, be sure to tell her I stopped by." *Oh, no. She didn't do a priest.*

Labor Day weekend came along with Mom, along with Alan, along with Mike. Yes, Mike and Mom had reunited in August, and he was now back in her good graces. I'm assuming for Mom it was an attempt to portray us as June and Ward Cleaver's All American family, albeit a somewhat dysfunctional one, to Alan.

All of us settled into a pattern: Mike working in RI weekdays while Miss Lynn ran the miles making sales calls. Alan and I were enjoying our senior year, while working together as busboys at Glastonbury Hills Country Club. Busting our butts on Friday and Saturday nights (plus special events), covering the entire dining room, we made a lot of money in tips allowing me to free up my week nights by leaving Maxwell's (which by now had been absorbed into the Adams Drug Store chain based in RI).

Never having had a sibling, I enjoyed having Alan as my at times younger, at times older brother. We shared an upstairs bedroom as my basement bedroom had been converted into our study/family room. It was tight quarters with a bed and a cot. Probably equally as tight as it was in Mom's room containing her bed and Mike's cot. *Right. Mike slept on the cot. Sure.*

I can honestly say Mom was fairly tame during the year Alan lived with us. She would even attempt to make a meal every so often, even though she agreed that her cooking was inedible at best. Let's just say Julia Child had nothing to worry about.

My dad was literally years behind in his child support payments when Mom finally contacted her Rhode Island attorney who brought the matter to family court. Mom drove to RI on the day of the hearing. She did not know that I skipped school that Friday and also drove to RI to attend. When I saw both parents with their lawyers at opposite ends of the hall in front of the courtroom, the scene struck me as totally absurd.

I went over to Mom and her attorney first and told them how insane it was to continue to battle it out twelve years after the divorce. She piped in, "Your father hasn't paid a cent in child support for the past eight years. He either comes up with the money or he's going to jail." After I told her she was doing fine financially without his money, she started screaming, "I don't care about the money. I want everyone to know how he didn't provide for his only son."

I walked over to my dad, wondering how Mom the Irrational and Dad the Thickheaded could have been married long enough to have me.

"Here's the deal, Dad. You agree to pick up the tab for my college, and Mom will drop her lawsuit, plus you'll never hear from her again." He said he would rather go to jail than to give that woman a nickel as she's nothing but a whore. I said what she is or is not is not the problem, the problem is you owe the money and she's not going to fold. His lawyer chimed in that he should take the deal because he was guaranteed to lose if the case was heard. My dad agreed.

Slowly walking back to my mother and her attorney, I tried to find the right words to assuage her vengefulness and get her to accept the deal. I told her paying for my college would be a lot more expensive than what she was seeking in back payments. She agreed. Then I added it would make a lot more sense if YOU forced Dad into paying for my college by dropping this lawsuit. At first she refused, wanting Dad to be annihilated on the stand. Her lawyer advised her that it would be in my best interest that SHE propose the deal. My mom agreed.

I went back to my dad and his counselor telling them it was a done deal and I had to get back to Connecticut to go to work. As I turned to leave, Dad's lawyer called me back, "Hey, Andy, with your skills, you should become a lawyer." I remember telling him, "No thanks; I have already had enough confrontation in my life."

Driving back home I patted myself on the back for brokering my first deal, fully realizing that my dad had no intention of ever paying for my college education. What surprised me is that Mom never mentioned that right after their divorce Dad had sold some real estate he and Mom had jointly owned. In exchange for Mom's signing the property over to him, Dad had (wait for it) promised to pay for my college education.

When the time came, I applied to two Connecticut colleges and Providence College. Having been accepted at all three, decision time had arrived. The gnawing priesthood feeling had also arrived once again. After church on a Sunday morning, I drove up to St. Albert's Carmelite Seminary in Middletown, New York. (Weird, huh, I was at the Carmelite junior seminary in Middletown, Massachusetts. Now I headed to Middletown, New York where their college seminary was located).

Spending the day prayerfully walking around the grounds, visiting their A-framed chapel, and being slobbered over by their gynormous Saint Bernard, I felt this was where I was being called to be.

The following day after school I called their vocation director and the following night I told Mom of my decision but instructed her this time, no black mantilla as it was a tad over the top. She said she was fine with whatever I did, and as long as I was happy she would be happy. Of course, my friend Alan had a different reaction, which began with "What kind of fucking lunatic are you…"

With our senior prom around the corner, I knew this would probably be my last date, for life. Unfortunately the girl I had dated throughout most of my high school years and I were not going to the prom together: She was going to the dance with a mutual friend and I had asked his former girlfriend who was also a mutual friend. I knew my former girlfriend was not happy about her dance partner, nor I mine. We all agreed to switch dates, and now she and I would be dancing together at our last high school prom.

With that snafu handled, what else could go wrong? Just as I was heading for the door to pick-up my date and another couple, Mom handed me a list of supermarket items she wanted me to pick-up before going to the prom. Standing in the kitchen dressed in my tux I told her I didn't have the time due to already being late to pick-up my date. She said unless I went shopping for her, I could not use *my* car that night. I called a friend who had graduated the previous year and within a few minutes I was behind the wheel of his car vowing never to accept anything as a gift from Mom - except maybe gold elf slippers but I'm getting way ahead of myself - as it always came with a string.

After our high school graduation, Alan was off to New York, Mom was off to her annual sales pilgrimage to northern New England, I was off to Rhode Island for the summer, and Mike…well, the Miss Lynn and Mike Show had come to an end for the second and final time.

5. Moving On

Whenever Mom and I would speak over the summer, I had a sense she was unhappy with her job. Her company had been bought out, and the new leadership and Miss Lynn were not speaking the same language: They spoke *corporate culture*, Mom spoke *I don't give a flying fuck about your corporate culture.*

"Can you imagine," she told me during one of these calls, "They made Adele my immediate supervisor. Adele, who lacks the intelligence to read a check correctly, and before I make any special arrangements with distributors it must first be reviewed by the Distributor Sales Department.

College started, and the next time I saw Mom was over Thanksgiving. She came to Rhode Island to celebrate the holiday with her family while I celebrated it with my dad's family.

After my first college semester at the seminary, we came to a mutual agreement that the priesthood was not for me, and I transferred to Pace University in the Wall Street area of New York City. Since Pace did not offer any student housing, Val managed through a brewery contact to obtain housing for me at the YM-YWHA (Young Men's and Young Women's Hebrew Association on 92nd Street). There were only two non-Jewish residents on the premises: A Baptist from Worcester, MA, and the Italian-Catholic fresh from the seminary. Oi.

Mom came to New York to take me to dinner with her new "friend", Jim, who owned a jewelry company in Providence. She was gushing about how they were partners in a new venture called *PerCent'Anni* (for a hundred years), which involved mounting a photograph taken at a special occasion onto a plaque and memorializing the event for a hundred years. It did not take until dessert to realize their partnership exceeded normal business hours. I made up some phony school related meeting I had to attend and took off.

The next day Mom called, outraged that I would be so rude to Jim, "After all, he did buy you dinner." I asked for his address in order to send him a check. She hung up.

I am guessing that Mom gave the new execs at the coloring company the same ultimatum she had been using so successfully for years: "If you don't like the way I'm handling your sales in New

England, then maybe you should get someone else." Which is exactly what they did.

Mom plotted her revenge and contacted competing hair color companies for employment. It appears that her reputation as a volatile, obstinate, out-of-control employee preceded her as she could not even get an interview.

Eventually moving back to Rhode Island, she opened Miss Lynn's Beauty Salon in East Providence. The small strip mall housing her salon would need a complete makeover to upgrade to shoddy. Mom's salon continued the motif with the sloppily painted sign over the front door, the extension cords dangling perilously from stained ceiling tiles, and the gaudy plastic shower curtain covering the doorway to the back room. Yet she had three "heads" under the dryers and more ladies waiting their turn to have Miss Lynn or Miss Bertha snazzy up their do's.

I have to once again give Mom credit; she was always the consummate wheeler dealer. Something was bringing in the "heads" to pack her slipshod hole-in-the-wall. After introducing me to her elderly clients, Mom excused herself and took me into the backroom. There I found a stack of badly printed fliers with the title "Golden Agers National Beauty Club" printed at the top over a sheet of coupons. The coupons were for discounts on the various hair services she offered. Bear in mind, this was in the early 70's, when housewives were still collecting Green Stamps and couponing was nowhere near as widespread as it is today.

Mom's vision was to expand her "Golden Agers Beauty Club" coupons to other salons across the area, the state, the world. According to her calculations, now that I was a sophomore in college I should know enough about all there is to know to help her get her latest venture off the ground. I explained I had no business experience but would be willing to stop back the following week to discuss it further.

I was eager to put distance between Miss Lynn's latest venture and me and get back to my Providence apartment, close to the campus of Providence College where I had transferred from Pace in New York City. Not bad, three colleges in two years. Guess by this stage in my life I had mastered the school transfer thing: Six elementary schools, two high schools, three colleges and counting.

Thankfully, Mom busied herself spiffying-up local senior citizens with her coupon promotions and said nothing more about her notion to create a national beauty club for golden agers. However she was not quite busy enough to stop making daily phone calls to leave messages on my answering machine.

Apparently, *normal* children call their mother once a day, the not-so-subtle implication being that I was not normal. Between being a full-time dean's list college student and working three-part time jobs to keep a roof over my head and Ramen Noodles on my table, I didn't have a lot of time to worry about it. The deal I struck in the hallway outside the family courtroom to end the delinquent child support feud between Mom and Dad had long since been forgotten. Dad did not contribute to my college education.

After graduation I received two full-time job offers, both of which came from companies where I was already working part-time. I chose a local ice cream company, Federal Ice Cream, as the one with the most opportunity for growth and advancement.

Mom felt as though I was throwing my life away and I would be much better off pursuing our renewed dream of making Golden Agers National Beauty Club a success. Wait - *our dream?*

6. GANBC

Although I was working at the ice cream company full-time I wanted to pursue my MBA (Master of Business Administration) degree at the University of Rhode Island's Providence campus on an evening and weekend basis. Returning to my apartment, most nights I would be greeted by my answering machine's flashing red light signaling there was a message or messages waiting for me. Nine times out of ten they would be from Miss Lynn. Typically they would sound like this:

Message 1: Rusty, it's urgent you call me. I have an idea.

Message 2: Rusty, I don't understand why you haven't called me back. I know you're there. Call me, it's an emergency.

Message 3: Well, Andrew [using "Andrew" ties me to the scorn she still felt toward my dad, her ex], I know you're avoiding my calls. Don't bother calling me back.

Phone slamming sound.

I would return her *urgent* calls after my Saturday classes. This became my strategy for calling Mom back: Call her on Saturdays at her salon when she was so busy with heads she would not have time to chat or discuss her latest and greatest game plan to conquer the world.

With Thanksgiving approaching, Mom did leave a message reminding me – as though I could forget – this Thanksgiving was hers. Although I was over twenty-one I would still loosely follow the court ordered holiday schedule granted to parents sharing custody of a child: Alternating holidays between she and Dad. If I spent Christmas with Dad, I'd spend Easter with Mom followed by Thanksgiving with Dad and so it went ever since I was five. Every holiday became a contentious tug-of-war until both parents died.

Rather than go through the hassle of making a turkey dinner for just the two of us, I suggested we go out for dinner. She agreed, knowing full well the last time she cooked our Thanksgiving dinner; the turkey was so dry sawdust would have been a moister alternative. *Scrambled eggs, please.*

From the moment she got in my car and through the drive to the restaurant, it was Golden Agers this, Golden Agers that. During dinner Mom said, "With your college education, and now with your MBA, I would think you would see this as the opportunity of your lifetime." I almost choked before I once again tried to explain what I had told her as a sophomore in college with slight variations: I was only a few months into a part-time MBA program and years away from getting the degree. As for this life-time opportunity to attract blue hairs into beauty salons, I was not convinced it was sustainable.

Then, as usual, an argument followed about how I was like "Big Andrew," who was stuck in the past, never attempting new ventures, and that I was wasting my time with getting an advanced degree, that I should just, "Open up a two-bit diner and variety store like your father." So much for wanting my opinion.

Somewhere on the road driving Mom back to her apartment from the restaurant, along with the silent treatment came the sniffles, indicating the water works had started. Once we arrived in front of her apartment, as she was exiting the car it was a curt, tearful, formal, "Good-bye, Andrew." In the same tone and with equal formality I said, "Good-bye, Mother." Door slam and I was granted at least a few weeks reprieve from Golden Agers National Beauty Club phone messages.

Mom invited me to a Christmas party for her beauty salon's hairdressers and customers. Oddly missing from my Christmas wish list that year was a party with a cluster of elderly ladies in front of a plastic shower curtain. Still, I decided to suck it up and stop by for a few minutes. It would not kill me, especially considering the alternative: phone calls and angry messages galore.

"Look everyone; this is my son, Rusty." Rusty. Great. (Mom started calling me Rusty when the Mom and Dad Show ended. She would claim it was because of my rust hair color. Thankfully I was not bald at age 5 as I am today otherwise my nickname would have been…well, you know.)

I looked around at the festively decorated salon and noticed the floral plastic shower curtain door to her backroom think tank had been replaced with a plastic shower curtain featuring Santa and his sleigh. Nice.

After a reasonably tolerable half-hour, I was inches from a clean getaway when Mom called me back and wanted to know when we could get together to talk about her Golden Agers. In my mind the instantaneous response was, "Never", even as I listened to myself say that, since I was off from graduate school for my semester break, we could get together most any night or a

Saturday. A valiant evasive try. "When?" she said. We finally settled for a couple of nights after Christmas. Then I hurriedly left the female senior citizen holiday zone.

I decided if I was able to demolish her concept of beautifying America's seniors once and for all, it would get me off the hook for any further nonsensical conversations. When we met over lunch, I dealt the dream-deflating blow: Beauty salons will not buy your program of giving senior citizen hair customers discounts via pieces of paper with coupons, when they could easily do it themselves for free.

"Okay, then, what do you suggest?" I knew she did not want to hear my suggestion to forget marketing Golden Agers to beauty salons. Or my suggestion to develop a way to market directly to the end users, the senior ladies themselves, and derive revenue from that source. I said it anyway.

Faster than I could say, "Check please," she rejected any idea of losing the coupons and deriving income from her seniors. About the only productive result of our marketing meeting was that Mom didn't raise the subject of Golden Agers with me for the next six months.

The following summer she called me at the ice cream company to set up another meeting. We met at the area's gastronomical palace, Harry's New York Hot Wiener System. She said she was burnt out running the beauty salon and wanted to throw herself into making Golden Agers a success. It was agreed we would get together for lunch the following week and I would come up with marketable ideas on how she could tap the senior citizen market.

The usual lunchtime crowd packed Harry's the following week, but Mom managed to grab a booth. After ordering, I pulled out an old "Dine Out Tonight" book, suggesting she pattern the Golden Ager business after them.

What Dine Out, a RI forerunner to the Entertainment Books, would do is sign-up restaurants to provide discount offers to anyone presenting the Dine Out coupon torn from their bound coupon books. It brought new business to the participating restaurants, and cost them nothing beyond the discount offer they provided to Dine Out customers.

I proposed her coupon booklet not only include beauty salons, but pharmacies, restaurants and various entertainment outlets like movie theaters, Newport mansion tours, local performances, etc. This would create the revenue stream she sought (from seniors joining her Golden Ager group by purchasing her coupon book). As long as the book had value to seniors, they would be willing to pay for it.

In the standard Mom Operations Manual of putting the cart before the horse, she was raring to go, saying she intended to sign up businesses on her way back to East Providence. I told her signing up businesses was like starting at step 9, when she has not completed Step 1 yet.

Step 1 should be to build the company's image with those businesses she would pitch to be included in the program. This would entail getting a small office having a downtown Providence address. I suggested one of the older office buildings as the rent would be inexpensive. Next step would be to create clean, easy to read (and recall) graphics. I gave her the name of a graphic designer I had used in the past.

After leaving Harry's, Mom headed into Providence and shopped for office space. Her choice was a relic of a building smack in the center of the city. A place so old and decrepit, it would have to undergo extensive renovations to barely qualify to be condemned. But, it was a downtown Providence address and that is all that mattered.

Within a few weeks, when the graphics were delivered to Mom, she called me to stop by the office in between work and night class. The building's squawking elevator only went to the second floor. From there you had to pass various decaying retail businesses and a beauty salon, closed for the day, but leaving behind a permeating aroma in the hall as a stinging-nasal reminder that they also offered their patrons permanents. A large creaking staircase in the middle of the building led to the third and fourth floors. I remember feeling grateful Mom's office was on the third floor.

Entering the Golden Agers office was interesting. A long bench of individually carved wooden seats, looking like it belonged on the altar of a cathedral rather than an office, lined the wall as I walked in. Turns out the seats *were* from a cathedral, Providence's

Sts. Peter and Paul Cathedral, and were junked when they remodeled the church. The rest of the offices were filled with the office furniture even the building's move-outs refused to take with them. None of this mattered as I anticipated no one would ever visit the office; just a downtown Providence address was required.

Mom was so excited at having put together her office in a couple of weeks, that when she asked what I thought of her new digs, I responded they were looking good. Unfortunately, when she showed me the graphic silhouette for her new logo, I could not be quite as upbeat. Instead of getting in touch with the graphic designer I suggested, Mom used the same "graphic designer" who had created the "Miss Lynn's Beauty Salon" sign, achieving similar chintzy results with the Golden Ager logo.

Although Mom was not all that pleased with the way the designer had illustrated my mom's mom, my nonne, who was to become the official symbol of Golden Agers, it was too late as Mom had already ordered letterheads, envelopes and business cards with the hideous image. I told her to trash them as she would never get a second chance to make a favorable first impression… especially when that initial impression was of a horse-headed shaped and emaciated granny.

My graphics person agreed to a rapid turnaround from the time Mom dropped Nonne's picture off to him to when he would have the final line art rendering ready. He was true to his word, and the graphic he created was true to the photograph of my smiling grandmother, chubby cheeks and all.

While this was going on, my two item contract for participating salons and other businesses expanded into over twenty clauses once Mom filled it with her demands, none of which made the final cut. Basically the only requirements participating businesses would have to agree to were (1) Honor their discount offer for one year, and (2) Make Golden Ager discount books available to their customers with a retail price of $5 from which they would earn $1.50 per sale.

Beyond obtaining the best printing rates, I had zero time to work with the printer to complete the book of coupons. I left that to Mom. Initially twenty-five businesses signed-up and the first printing run was set at one thousand books at the price of ninety-three cents per book, which would sport a glossy black cover with the Great Agers name and logo scripted in luxurious gold ink.

A week later after the books were delivered, I made a lunchtime visit to check them out. My obvious shock did not even cause a blip on Mom's radar.

"I said glossy black cover with gold ink."

Mom blithely said black was so blah, she decided a matte gold cover would be a better choice, since it would better tie in with the name Golden Agers.

"I guess that's why you also went with the unreadable yellow ink on top of the flat gold cover."

I was disgusted. Paging through the book I noticed additions for discounts to purchase wigs, bottles of hair coloring and other items such as stuffed animals for their grandchildren: All may be purchased at Miss Lynn's Hair Salon, Bullocks Point Avenue, East Providence.

I placed the book back in its box and bluntly told her to not run any more business ideas by me or ask for my opinion again, since it was obvious she would do what she wanted anyway.

"But what's wrong with them?" she wondered.

"Do you really think any sane salon owner will promote these books as long as your beauty salon, their competitor, is plastering coupons all over it? And while you're at it, tell me which pharmacy will promote this book, which is clearly trying to steal their hair coloring business from them. You never listen to anyone."

Mom proceeded to advise me that she was in business before I was born (ah, yes, our fabled family enterprise) and has the street smarts to always know what is best.

During her fervent efforts, visiting senior centers and senior apartment complexes over the next three or four months, Mom claimed she sold 150 books while the other salons and retailers only sold "a couple." I found the 150 sold books claim dubious at best. Holding a drawing at each senior gathering and giving away 2 or 3 free books to the lucky winners? Now that was more her style.

Sensing a consolidation in the ice cream business in which the big guys would come in and gobble up small local struggling manufacturers, I left Federal Ice Cream to open my own marketing business, concentrating on new product development.

Guess who wanted to be my first client?

The first words out of Mom's mouth specified that she wanted to be treated like any other client and, unlike before, she would pay for my services. I reiterated how I could not work with her. She would do what she wanted, when she wanted, which would be a complete waste of my time and energy.

I consented to meet with her for one time and one time only to talk about Golden Agers. If she blew off my advice and did not immediately implement my recommendations, there would not be a second Golden Agers meeting.

We met, and I said that the name Golden Agers National Beauty Club was too narrow in terms of products as well as its customer base, namely female senior citizens. This left 50% of that demographic – men – out of the equation entirely. I said that until a more suitable name was developed, the company should go under the acronym GANBC (Gan-bic). Surprisingly, she agreed.

Making GANBC into a limited, membership only club would (hopefully) encourage people to join for the many free benefits she would provide. Again, Mom agreed.

Next on my agenda was to determine revenue streams for GANBC. I identified two areas which were tracking positively for seniors: Insurance and travel. After meeting with a few insurance brokers, they recommended that GANBC members be offered life insurance policies rather than health insurance. One broker told me: Life insurance is an easier sell; the person is either dead or not dead.

Travel proved to be a natural fit for seniors who had the time and money to spend vacationing.

GANBC was taking shape. No revenue would be derived from seniors joining GANBC and enjoying discounted offers from area businesses. Revenue would only flow to GANBC by seniors taking its trips.

Going the route of marketing tours to GANBC members presented two problems: Mom lacked travel experience, and some seniors would not be able to climb the stairs to get to her office to book their trips. I suggested she find a travel agency where she could rent desk space where GANBC members could come and meet with her and feel secure in plunking down their money while booking their trips, and she would also be acquiring travel knowledge and skills.

Mom met with Tony, who had recently purchased Aylsworth Travel in Providence. He said that he had another location on the other side of Providence on Broadway called Broadway Travel, where he would be willing to let her have an office rent free as long as all air ticketing for her trips be processed through Aylsworth. Mom's last two problems were solved.

Staffing would not be a problem. Tony's office staff at his Broadway location was well versed in handling travel. It was an ideal situation for Mom, since there were people who could answer her telephone lines while she was out promoting GANBC at senior meetings.

Over the next couple of years GANBC grew largely as a result of addressing senior groups, giving away free memberships to take advantage of area discounts, and word-of-mouth. Whenever we would promote a trip, at least fifty to a hundred people would make reservations.

With this kind of volume, travel vendors were calling us, and we no longer had to chase and convince them to let us sell their tours.

Because my days were being partially filled consulting over GANBC matters, I decided to take advantage of the offer Tony made me to move my marketing office to the mostly vacant third floor of the Broadway location. A couple of months prior to this Mom had moved into the apartment behind the first floor offices in an effort to spend more time on the business and less on commuting.

One day an American Airlines representative, knowing of our growth and travel volume, met with us and asked us to consider chartering one of their planes to fly a group that we would put together to anywhere American flew. Bear in mind, this was at a time when airlines had a large number of excess planes and were eager to have a company like GANBC help utilize a surplus plane's downtime. Mom and I discussed this extremely ambitious project since it would involve filling a plane with 184 paid passengers.

While considering American's offer, we continued to market and fill our air tour blocks at a self-imposed limit of a hundred GANBC passengers per trip. It became impractical for Mom to be the tour escort traveling with each group, even with the assistance of one or two other tour coordinators. She now began to concentrate on expanding the number of GANBC tour escorts we would have at our disposal.

Instead of having to push our way into senior centers to pitch GANBC membership and travel, senior centers started contacting us and welcoming our representatives. It was during this period that Mom met an executive director of a neighborhood center who would become the next man of her dreams.

Len (not to be confused with the Lenny previously mentioned) Simmons and Mom began dating. He was a fun loving guy and it was not long before the Miss Lynn and Len Show began with him moving in with her. Besides being even-tempered and stable, he was eager to assist Mom with keeping herself organized. He was also willing to take vacation time from his job to escort a traveling GANBC group. Whatever Lynn wanted, Len was most accommodating.

Mom's brother, my Uncle Ernie, was also willing to take time from his auto parts sales job and escort tours whenever needed. Sending Len and my uncle out on tour together was perfect, as they were both lively and fun-loving, and from a financial perspective, they could room together, saving the cost of paying for separate rooms for a male and female tour escort. In addition to this, the two guys became instantaneous friends.

Although Mom was convinced she was the most organized person ever created, the reality was she was not even within hailing distance. Yet she insisted on handling all of the mundane matters like passenger manifests and rooming lists herself. Invariably, lists would be sent incorrectly: Passenger names on Tour "A", would be mixed up with passenger names on Tour "B," thereby causing chaos for the escorts when checking their groups into hotels. Incorrect names and incorrect room assignments were all too common.

Whenever I would bring these problems to Mom's attention, she would tell me she had to fill in random names forty-five days before the group's arrival in order to meet the hotel's rooming list due date. Otherwise the hotel might release rooms. I could accept that, but when I questioned her as to why she did not call the hotels to revise their list with the late booking new names and remove the incorrect names, she would get agitated and respond, "You cannot expect me to do everything." No, I do not expect you to do everything, I told her, what I do expect is that you will let someone else handle that for you in the interest of accuracy.

It all came to a head when Mom's organizational skills were tested by a tour group headed to Miami Beach under the leadership of Len and Uncle Ernie. Her fudged rooming list caused pandemonium at the hotel once it was understood that not a single passenger of the hundred member tour had a name matching the rooming list sent to them by Mom. As if this situation could not be made worse, the hotel was sold out. There was no flexibility in terms of additional rooms needed or fulfilling room requests like rooms next to each other or for those having special needs.

Our phones were blazing with passengers calling from Miami seeking to return home and passenger relatives notifying us of the chaotic situation. The office staff knew it was better to avoid having Miss Lynn take any of these disgruntled calls, due to her tendency to scream back at all the unhappy travelers and their families.

In an effort to smooth a whole lot of ruffled feathers, I decided to take the first available flight to Miami before the passengers decided to fly home and lodge complaints against us with consumer groups and/or the media.

Arriving at the hotel in the late afternoon, I found Len and Uncle Ernie in the lobby, looking frazzled after seven or so hours of being berated by our unhappy tour group members. When Uncle Ernie spotted me entering the lobby, he called out, "We're saved! The Seals have arrived!"

Within a couple of hours, we had everyone in their rooms and were even able to honor special requests for adjacent or adjoining rooms. By now, I was not sure if *we* had rooms, but the passengers were happy and that was all that mattered.

I ordered a meet and greet wine and cheese get together for later that night. The next day the three of us made it our goal to seek out each passenger and see if there was anything we could do for them to make their Miami vacation more enjoyable.

Len and Uncle Ernie decided to take whoever wanted to join them for dinner to a well known Miami restaurant. I opted not to go as I had to be at the airport by seven the next morning in order to return to Rhode Island for a noontime meeting. Half the group wanted to go so I authorized chartering a bus for the night.

I was in bed by 9 and probably asleep by 9:01, when the phone rang. I looked at the clock and saw it was 12:45AM. Uncle Ernie was calling to tell me that a couple of women did not make it to the bus at 11 when they sent the rest of the passengers back to the hotel. He said he and Len had been searching for the ladies for almost two hours and were now desperate. I asked the missing passengers' names and the name of the club where the ladies were last seen.

When I gave the cab driver the club's name and street address, he turned around and said, "Buddy, you sure?" I told him I was.

He eventually pulled up in front of a brightly lit club with "Salute to Broadway" on its marquee. As I was getting out of the cab, the driver asked if I wanted him to wait. I said to not bother, as I had to go find a couple of ladies. He snickered.

Once inside the darkened club, my ears were assaulted by disco-styled show tunes played at ear-piercing levels. The place was packed with women; some looked like they were costumed in Hello Dolly get ups. After my eyes adjusted to the lights, I felt weird as I saw a great number of eyes staring at me. It finally hit me: This is a drag bar.

I bolted out the front door and was greeted by Len and Uncle Ernie, who were laughing like hyenas. Furious, I walked past the two pranksters and jumped back into the same cab I'd taken earlier, which, fortunately for me, he had not picked up his next fare.

The cabbie said to me, "Them ladies ain't your type?"

Len and my uncle tried to join me in the cab to return to the hotel. Um, no, I don't think so.

Later in the day when I was back in my office picking up the messages left while I was "enjoying" Miami, Mom came out of her back office and asked if there was anything I wanted to tell her. What was there to tell? Problems were solved, angry passengers were happy. What she wanted to know about was my penchant for drag bars when I travel. Len and Uncle Ernie, both of you are dead when you get back.

We then proceeded to another blowout over her clerical skills, or lack thereof, causing a calamity and forcing me to hop on the first flight to Florida. Her utter incompetence and refusal to give up control of clerical duties, as I had suggested, nearly led to the ruin of the company's reputation (and bye-bye business after that). Miss Lynn remained unmoved.

When Team Len and Ernie finally got back to the office to turn in their paperwork, they walked in wearing "old lady hats," complete with fake fruit and mesh pulled down over their faces.

I was pretty sure that everyone in the office was in on the prank, since I could see them stifling their laughter and trying to gauge my reaction. Glancing over at the two culprits, I walked over to Uncle Ernie, made a minor adjustment to his hat, and said, "Much better, Sweetie," before slapping his butt and exiting the office for the serenity of the third floor.

While I maintained GANBC should be first and foremost a membership organization with travel as a benefit but not the only benefit, Mom persisted in promoting only travel when speaking before senior groups instead of also telling them about the discounts we were able to provide GANBC members. It was my contention that expanding the discount program would lead to the sustainability and growth of the organization, as well as more of a membership base to market travel.

It was agreed we would offer one major tour to a different destination every other month or if the demand was there, each month. This would add a variety of exciting places for our members to visit.

Prior to leaving for a business trip shortly after I got back from Miami, Mom and I met and planned the major fall and winter trips for the remainder of the year. Our focus in the near term was filling the plane we chartered from American Airlines to Acapulco which was scheduled to depart the beginning of May.

When I returned I learned Mom had signed a contract for a tour to Spain's Costa del Sol's Torremolinos located on the Mediterranean Sea by inexplicably moving its scheduled September dates to the second week of May. Only problem was, the Acapulco full-plane tour was the first week of May.

Despite it being only a week since the contract was signed, the tour operator claimed the hefty deposit Mom made would be forfeited should we cancel or reschedule. With less than three months to go, the Acapulco trip was short by fifty passengers, and the Spain trip was not even close to being marketed to the membership.

As the departure dates approached, I questioned Mom as to which tour escorts she was considering for each tour. She would head the five member tour operation staff to Acapulco, and Len and Uncle Ernie would take the Spain tour. I disagreed with her decision, stating it's one thing for those two to have problems in the U.S., but internationally?

A week before the charter to Acapulco was scheduled to depart, Mom came up to my office with a terrified look on her face. It seems that she had had a premonition the Acapulco trip would be problematic and pleaded with me to take her place. After a few stipulations, such as an accurate rooming list to be called in to the hotel at least 48 hours prior to our arrival, and selecting my own tour escorting staff to travel with me, I consented. Shortly after she returned to her office, she called to tell me I would have to take the four support staff she selected, as she already told them of their Mexico assignment. In that case, I responded, reassign yourself to head the tour as well.

Mom caved, and I kept two of the staffers she had already selected and replaced the other two with very strong escorts. In retrospect, it was a good thing I did.

All went smoothly as we boarded the plane and buckled up for our exciting Mexico vacation. Waiting for the door of the aircraft to be secured, I was surprised to see it reopen as the airline representative we dealt with for this charter came aboard and approached me. He asked the lead flight attendant to verify with the other members of the flight crew that there were no available seats. I asked him what was up and he told me Mom had overbooked the tour and more passengers were waiting at the gate to board. Looks like Miss Lynn is going to have a lot of 'splainin' to do.

This was probably an omen.

After a few minutes, the door closed again, and the next time it opened, we were in Acapulco.

Leading a group through customs and immigration is pretty routine, especially if it's a tour group of seniors. I was one of the first to be processed, since I had to make sure there were five buses waiting curbside to transport everyone to our hotel. Once verified, I assigned two of my tour escorts to handle the loading process outside while I headed back to the security area to make sure everyone had been processed into the country. As I walked back our American Airlines Acapulco representative came rushing toward me. Apparently one inebriated female passenger thought it would be hilarious to tell the agent processing her that she had a gun with her for "self-protection". Security failed to see her humor and would not allow her to enter the country. She was brought to one of their detention rooms.

The only way I could reach the detention area was to present my passport and "leave" the Mexico side of security which I did. Seeing my two remaining tour escorts at the end of our passenger lines I instructed them to tell our other escorts who were boarding the passengers outside the terminal to fill all the buses and double check head counts and then proceed to the hotel to get settled in while I waited for *Annie Oakley* to clear immigration. Once I was able to spring her, we would take a taxi to the hotel.

It took over an hour to get her released.

Since my passport stamps indicated I had entered their country and exited their country a little more than an hour ago, I could only imagine how suspect I looked. The security officers who detained the woman explained the circumstances to the Mexican immigration officer to no avail. In order to add a new entry stamp to my passport, he would have to clear it with his supervisor who was in a meeting (aren't they always). After some back and forth between immigration and security, the entry agent let us into Mexico, under the condition that I leave my passport with him while he cleared the reentry stamp with his superior. After that, someone would personally deliver my passport to me at the hotel. Relieved to be free to go, I did not have a problem with this.

During the cab ride, my liquored up tour member was sobering and crying. If I'd known what awaited me at the hotel, I would have followed her lead and liquored up myself.

The lobby was full of our passengers sitting on their luggage, on the floor and, for some lucky ones, on lobby seating. I looked over at the long registration desk and noticed four orange caped GANBC women speaking with seven or eight hotel staffers. As I crossed to the desk, I recall a random woman making a nasty comment to me about this tour being a disaster. Couldn't agree with you more, lady.

Working off the rooming lists we each had with us, the hotel was feverishly attempting to reconcile the list that had been called into them with the passengers sitting in their lobby. It appeared the wrong list was called into the hotel, and the rooms were therefore assigned incorrectly. Shocking! How could something like this happen?

I called over to the front desk manager and suggested we work off my master list, as it was probably the most accurate. We would then write the room numbers next to who was rooming with whom; they could always update the new info into their system after our passengers were settled. He agreed and within forty minutes, the lobby was cleared of our planeload of vacationers.

We, along with the hotel front desk crew, started from scratch to input names and room assignments into the hotel's system. It was after 2AM when we finished.

Because of it being so late, I relieved bleary eyed Elsa, one of our staff, from the responsibility of accompanying a City Tour of Acapulco which was scheduled to leave the hotel in six hours. I would escort it instead.

According to our office roster, 27 of our passengers had elected to take this optional tour. When I arrived in the hotel lobby, there were 43 GANBC members anxiously waiting to enjoy the Acapulco City Tour. Some unlisted people had their receipts signed by Miss Lynn, herself. Others not on the list insisted they had paid Mom for this full day excursion. The ground tour operator we contracted called their dispatcher, and a 49 passenger motor coach was sent to replace the 30 passenger coach sitting in front of the hotel. Additional luncheon meals were called in to accommodate the extra passengers.

One of the stops along this tour was to see the cliff divers. Once there, I located a pay telephone and called our office. I asked for Maureen and brought her up-to-date on everything that had happened so far. She wanted to transfer my call to Miss Lynn, but I refused to talk with Mom and insisted on Maureen personally checking the records in an effort to update and correct the remaining optional tour lists.

The real challenge would be the accuracy of the passenger manifest for the next day's Mexico City excursion, which involved a flight from Acapulco to Mexico City. If some of our passengers were not ticketed, we would have major problems at the airport. Maureen agreed to work on this tour first and contact Elsa back at the hotel with any additions or corrections while I was out on the current day trip. (While there I should have filled out an application to become a cliff diver. Couldn't be any more dangerous than leading a tour organized by Miss Lynn.)

When our coach arrived back at the hotel later that afternoon, Elsa was waiting for me at the curb. As I jovially greeted each disembarking passenger, Elsa whispered to me while also smiling at our returning city tour passengers that Maureen had called with an updated passenger list for the air tour to Mexico City. Not only were there many errors in already ticketed passenger names (which would present a problem at the airport, because their ID's would not match the airline's passenger manifest), but the actual count of those who paid for the tour numbered 86 and not the 71 we had on our list.

At this point I was sure the ground operator regretted ever doing business with GANBC but came to the hotel in order for everything to (hopefully) go seamlessly the next day. Overnight, tickets had to be issued for the unaccounted for passengers and reissued for the wrongly named passengers. Madeline, another of my tour coordinators who would be in charge of the Mexico City bound passengers, was briefed about the problems, and I decided to accompany the group to the airport in the event there were any other unexpected mess-ups.

Six of these mess-ups were standing in front of us when we were about to board the awaiting coaches to transfer the group to the airport. Their names were neither on our original list nor on Maureen's updated list. Two of them had their receipts with them signed by, drum roll please, Miss Lynn.

You can imagine my relief when the week was over and I hopped on board Bus 5 to take us all to the airport for our return flight home. Using my driver's license as an ID since my passport had not been returned to me at the hotel, I was the last of our GANBC visitors to officially leave the Mexico side of the terminal.

The older agent who processed me was kind enough to assure me that he would personally track down my passport and see to it that it was sent to me. He probably has long since died of natural causes, and I'm still without that particular passport.

Our plane landed in Dallas to process us through U.S. customs and immigration before continuing to Rhode Island.

It was a little after midnight when we finally made our way to the baggage claim area and found Miss Lynn waiting to welcome everyone back home. One of my escorts turned to me and said, "Look, Andy, your mom is greeting all us little people." In spite of being exhausted, upset and sick with a virus, I still found her remark hilarious.

As soon as Mom caught sight of me, she headed in my direction, but not to greet me, mother to son. No, she wanted to tell me about the many passengers who told her what a great time they had. I said nothing. She added that since there were no problems, just as she had perceived, she should have led the tour herself. I walked away. Calling after me, she wanted to know what my problem was. I turned around and said "You," before continuing to my car in long term parking.

Driving home, I resolved to never set foot in the first floor offices again. Ever. Let Mom do her own thing, her way, until GANBC ultimately collapses under her delusion of being the most organized woman of the century. I also determined it would probably take most of the week to shake my virus related sore throat and bodily aches, as well as my exhaustion.

After what seemed like only a few hours sleep, probably because it was only a few hours sleep, my phone rang. It was Maureen. She had stopped by the office after seeing our Spain group's airport bound buses off and found messages from the hotel in Spain. I interrupted her and said, "Wrong rooming list, right?" She said what she thought had happened was Miss Lynn mixed up the Acapulco list with the Spain list, because we only had a room block of around 50 rooms in Spain, while the list furnished to them by Miss Lynn called for 97 rooms.

I reminded Maureen of my call to her about the rooming list mix-up while I was on the Acapulco City Tour. She reminded me who was leading the Spain tour: Len and Uncle Ernie.

I immediately went to the office.

Working from the air passenger manifest, we pieced together who was rooming with whom. While Maureen was on the phone with the hotel calling in passenger names and room requirements, I decided to verify the accuracy of the optional tours, which involved the painstaking auditing of individual passenger reservation forms. It did not take me long to realize the optional tour lists, which were now in the hands of Len and Uncle Ernie, were totally incorrect. (Not to mention those optional tours booked but never having made it to any reservation form as I experienced the previous week.)

When their buses reached Kennedy Airport (NYC) on the first leg of their trip, they called into the office to update us. We brought them up to speed with what was going on. Maureen told them she had already contacted the hotel with an accurate rooming list, so they should not have any problem at check-in. I filled them in on the optional tours and instructed them to disregard the lists they had with them. Maureen would call in new lists once they arrived in Torromolimos.

A couple of minutes after the call, the office door banged open and an irate Miss Lynn stormed in. "Who do you think you are?" she bellowed. "You have no right telling Len and my brother that my lists were wrong." Not even bothering to look up or respond, I continued searching the reservation forms for booked optional tours. "I'm talking to you, junior."

Being used to these displays, I paid no attention, but it shocked Maureen.

"Your son is sick, running on a few hours sleep, and in here saving your ass the way he did last week down in Acapulco. Leave us alone so we can prevent another Miss Lynn catastrophe in another foreign country this week."

Mom charged out of the office, and we spent the rest of the day researching and reconstructing all the optional excursions. Maureen said she would be in the office early the next morning when the tour group would be arriving at their hotel at 1PM, or 7AM our time. I said I would be taking a few days off.

Around 10 the next morning Maureen called to tell me there was an emergency and I needed to get to the office. Len had just called in from the airport. There was a revolution of some sort going on in Portugal, and their plane was forced to land and be searched before they could continue using Portugal's air space on their way to Spain. A revolution? Why not?

Walking into the office I could sense panic in the air as the phones continued ringing off the hook: Concerned relatives having received SOS calls from their loved ones from the airport in Portugal were eager to know that they were safe.

In Portugal, our passengers were forced to deplane. They and their luggage were randomly searched for weapons or any kind of contraband. I quipped to Maureen, "Nothing spells revolution like a bunch of seniors flying overhead, tossing their empty Ensure cans out of the plane's windows."

Mom came out of her office. She had already forgotten her words of the previous day, as she informed me that we had a problem. *There's that "we" again.* As we sat in her office, she began to recount Len's conversation with her and how our passengers wanted to return home to America immediately. She said someone would have to go over to Spain to calm the situation and our passengers down.

I was positive that if she went over, it would be like dropping a keg of dynamite along with a 55 gallon drum of gasoline on an already blazing fire. And should some irate passenger cross swords with Miss Lynn, her wrathful response would make the revolution in Portugal pale by comparison.

My cousin, Jackie, happened to stop by the office and witnessed our dilemma.

Besides being sicker than sick, I was feeling relieved to get off the hook of salvaging the Spain trip once I realized my passport was still vacationing in Acapulco. It would take me weeks to get another.

"No, Andy, you can go to Boston's immigration office to get a replacement passport within an hour or so," Jackie said.

"I can't drive there, I'm too sick."

"Not a problem, I'll drive."

Of course you would.

As I was leaving, one of the office workers asked if I would be visiting my grandmother in Italy while in Europe. Apparently Mom had told all of the office staffers that my Italian grandmother still resided in Italy and presided over a cosmetic empire built on her youthful skin cream formulations. All I said was that I would not be visiting my grandmother while overseas. Not technically a lie since my grandmother was residing where she had always lived, in nearby Pawtucket, RI. Nonne's only formulation was a to-die-for spaghetti sauce.

The beauty of the Mediterranean Sea coupled with our beachfront hotel did much to calm the passengers' nerves. Of course, the sangria party we held after I arrived didn't hurt.

Over the following months, Mom continued to operate GANBC Travel as I continued to expand my marketing/advertising business.

At the beginning of the fall, Mom and Len got married.

Mom and I decided to pool our resources and buy an investment property, where she and Len could live and conduct GANBC business. After scouring available real estate in Greater Providence we found such a house. It was a large, 19-room Victorian on an oversized parcel of land, and also included a separate carriage house. In the future, Mom would crowingly refer to the property as The Big House, which occupied an entire corner and bordered three streets.

She and I formed GANBC Realty to purchase the house from M. DeRobbio & Sons, which had been using the basement office to run their Italian food importing business. The carriage house was in use as their warehouse, but they were currently in the process of expanding to larger quarters. The only remaining "& Sons" from the original M. DeRobbio & Sons was a lovely elderly woman named Ermelina. The property's closing was scheduled for December 1st.

The celebration of Mom and Len's marriage and the purchase of a new house was cut short when there was a massive fire at the Broadway location of GANBC, Mom's apartment, and my business. The building was condemned and scheduled to be razed. I was grateful most of the file cabinets survived.

Suitable temporary office space was secured directly across the street from the burned out property. And Ms. DeRobbio graciously allowed the closing to be advanced so that Len and Mom would have a place to move to: The Big House.

7. The Big House

Soon after Lynn and Len were settled in The Big House, the GANBC business also moved in. Trips now replaced the ziti and rigatoni being sold from the nondescript basement offices.

Years later, my wife discovered a note from "Mother Cooke" to her son requesting a meeting prior to his leaving for school the following morning. Investigating further, we learned that the house and property - an anachronism, considering the neighborhood was mostly populated with cottages and multi-family homes - was known as the Cooke Estate a number of owners ago. It had belonged to the Cooke family who owned and operated some sort of textile mill in nearby Olneyville.

You might wonder why a twenty-something would move back home after enjoying the independence of college and then living on his own. The answer was to save money. Since coming up with my share of the down payment on The Big House, I was financially drained. Remaining in my own apartment and renting high-priced downtown Providence office space was foolish considering I could save on both by utilizing a portion of the 19 rooms. My office would fill the entire third floor, which provided four times the space as downtown, and I could live in the studio apartment at one end of the second floor. The commute was ideal: 13 or 14 stairs.

A couple of months after settling in with our businesses and our lives, we held our first family meeting. These meetings usually turned into business meetings for Miss Lynn's business, rather than what they were intended to be, discussions about the property. Diverting the conversation, she would drone on about how her business needed my marketing expertise - as opposed to her husband's advice – and the session would abruptly end in a shouting match. Len would pout, because Mom never listened to him, and Mom wouldn't let Len forget that he, along with all the rest of us, lacked her business acumen. Sorry, Len, Miss Lynn wins. I bet you never had a plastic shower curtain concealing a think tank in the back room of your social service center.

Needless to say, rarely did anything get accomplished property-wise.

One meeting started with Mom insisting we install an in-ground swimming pool between The Big House and the carriage house. I was vehemently opposed to the idea, because I knew who would have pool cleaning duty, me. The Sovereign Nation of Miss Lynn being a democracy held an election. Three votes were cast: Two pro-pool and one opposed.

Although my vote had drowned, I did tell my fellow citizens that before they had the area between the house and carriage house excavated; they needed to check with the City of Providence to find out where our sewer lines were. (This was before organizations like "Dig Safe" came into existence.) Len assured me he'd make sure it was done, and we agreed to get together the following week after three bids were collected to select the company to handle the installation.

On the following Monday morning, as I backed my car down the circular driveway for a packed day of meetings, I looked to my right and saw Lynn, Len and a hard-hatted man holding what appeared to be plans in his hands. Great, I thought, someone from the city is tracking the sewer lines.

When I returned home that night, there was a backhoe sitting in the proposed pool area with a mountain of freshly dug sand alongside of it. I levitated out of my seat and stormed into the house. Spotting Len, I demanded to know what the hell was going on. He said, "Talk to your mother, you know how impulsive she is."

I found her in her basement office. "What's going on with the pool?"

"John was able to start the job today and he gave us a really good price."

"Wait a minute," I fumed. "We had a deal to get three quotes and make our decision next week."

"John just put in a pool next door to a friend's house. He stopped by this morning to talk about it. If you weren't in such a hurry to leave, you could have joined us to discuss it."

My head was pounding. "I thought that guy was from the city, making sure we wouldn't be digging up any sewer lines."

"As you can see, all the dirt's been removed and no sign of any sewer line."

A week later the pool was completed. Returning to my studio apartment overlooking the pool area, I glanced out the window, saw the water looked inviting, and decided to take a quick dip before getting ready to go out with friends.

After I dove in, I noticed the pool's vinyl liner under the diving board was pulling away from the side of the pool. Worse than this, I could stand in the deep end on a mound protruding from the same side. It made no sense, the pool was supposed to be twelve feet deep at that spot not five feet. I hopped out of the water to check out the cement pool apron which appeared normal. When I glanced over the newly planted shrubs, I noticed frothy foam-like water trickling onto the grass below the contoured mound of the new retaining wall constructed to accommodate the pool. I ran down to examine it further. It smelled like detergent.

Len was on the first floor when I found him and asked him to come outside with me. En route to that side of the house I asked him if anyone was washing clothes. He said he threw in a load of towels. As we reached where his rinse cycle was leaching, I turned to him and said, "I know."

"Oh, Christ. The godammed sewer line ruptured. They probably damaged it putting in the pool," he said as more foamy water gushed out.

Lynn was in her basement office, but hearing the commotion she came out to see what was going on.

While the two of them remained outside arguing with each other as to who was to blame for hiring the pool installing hack, I went inside to call the hack. At the very least I expected a contrite, slick business person anxious to correct this horrendous boo-boo. Instead, Mr. Hack became enraged and claimed it wasn't his fault because he installed the pool exactly where Miss Lynn insisted it be placed.

When there was finally a lull, I simply told him that if he and a crew weren't at our place within the hour, I was calling the Department of Business Regulation to have his pool contractor license pulled. The discharge from the washing machine proved he neglected to consult any agency in the City of Providence before the pool's installation.

Outside, Lynn and Len continued their shouting match. Now it was getting personal. They were not only arguing about Mr. Hack's incompetent stupidity, but each others.

As soon as Mr. Hack arrived, I told him the number one priority was to restore the ruptured sewer line to be fully functional by nightfall. Mom immediately contradicted me and demanded her pool be restored first, as this was her top priority. When she was finished, I reiterated where I wanted Mr. Hack (a/k/a Cheap Pool Guy) to start before turning to her and saying, "Unless you want the neighbors to know when you're washing a dish or taking a crap, the wolf at the door is the fucking sewer line."

As I walked away she started screaming, "Don't use that language in front of me, I am your mother. Where are you going? Don't you walk away from me!"

I got in my car and was looking to exit the lower entrance to the driveway, when I noticed Len getting into his car and exiting from the upper driveway. Seeing me, he just shook his head as I thought she is a lot more than you bargained for.

There were frequent parties at The Big House. Miss Lynn would invite Bertha (a former beautician at Miss Lynn's former beauty salon) and Elsa, who worked for GANBC and (as I later discovered) wasn't getting paid. Instead, Miss Lynn was awarding her earned "points" that only Miss Lynn herself knew the value of, and Elsa was waiting to earn enough points for a "free" vacation. An added bonus was that Elsa would also be "permitted" to be a tour guide! Without pay, of course, because, you know, you were on a free trip. Bertha and Elsa would come to Mom's parties, not as friends and guests, but as pseudo servants to serve the drinks and hors d'oeuvres to the other guests.

If I felt obligated to attend, I would invite a few of my friends. Actually I would bribe them with free drinks and food. Whenever the festivity was held inside, almost on cue after the last guest had arrived, Miss Lynn would descend the grand front staircase to the spacious foyer below, dressed to the hilt and exemplifying the theme of the party. When the gatherings were held outside, the side staircase was substituted so that she could still make her entrance before descending to graciously greet the common folk waiting below. Invariably, she would be wearing a large tiara. Her Majesty, Miss Lynn, Queen of the Universe.

It was not unusual for her to recolor her already dyed blond hair to suit the occasion. Christmas, bright red. Halloween, orange and black. But regardless of color, she would always wear the tiara.

The bartender at these extravaganzas would usually be an acquaintance, who would be flattered into duty. "No one can make (insert alcoholic beverage here) like you do, would you mind..."

One time I caught Len refilling the empty expensive bottles of liquor with stomach rotting, one step above rubbing alcohol, cheap store brands. When he saw me, he explained this was all my mother would let him buy. Note to self: Warn my friends to only drink bottle-capped beer.

Mom's persona at these soirees was, "I'm Miss Lynn and you're not." Watching her, I'd be reminded of Carol Burnett's portrayal of Norma Desmond. She had all the imperiousness along with the same striking obliviousness to present reality.

Even though we were living and working under the same roof, encounters with Mom were rare.

I met a girl and after my first date with Kathy, I knew she was the one for me. The next morning I dropped by the lower office to share this with everyone. That night Kathy and I went to dinner, and for dessert I brought her to my father's house, where all of his family had gathered to celebrate his birthday.

A month passed, and knowing she was the girl of my dreams, I felt in a sort of perverse way that it was time for Kathy to meet Miss Lynn.

We drove to The Big House. En route I was desperately searching for the right words to describe Mom without terrifying Kathy into jumping out of the car and running for her life. Truthfully, I was unsure which Miss Lynn would be joining us for dinner.

Introductions went smoothly, and only a minor skirmish as to whether Len or Mom was going to drive to dinner marred the beginning of the evening. As usual, Mom came out the winner and took the wheel.

After an uneventful dinner and ride back to The Big House, I explained that Kathy was a teacher and had school the next day, so I'd be driving her straight home. Mom insisted we come into the house and have a quick cup of coffee.

While waiting for the coffee to brew, we sat out on the back deck. The conversation was innocuous, though this could change instantaneously if Mom went off on a tangent or, God forbid, got all *Who's Afraid of Virginia Wolfe* on Len.

In the distance I heard a plane, which was not unusual given that we lived approximately fifteen miles from the airport. Minutes passed as the sound of the plane droned on in the background. Please God, let the coffee be done.

Mom asked, "Do you hear that?"

I shrugged and said, "No, not really."

She uttered to Kathy in a near whisper, "That's a UFO."

I glanced at Kathy who was staring at me with a please get me out of here look. I assured Mom, "It's only a plane."

"No, it's a UFO. Don't you remember when you were only a child and I took you to Florida? I saw a UFO hovering over the beach. They even reported it in the local newspaper."

I shot a pleading glance at Len. His facial response was, I have to live with her, buddy, you're on your own.

Suddenly Mom got up and went to the kitchen wall phone inside the deck's doorway. We all were silent, though my inner voice was saying, Jesus, take me now. Len did murmur, "Get ready for this."

"Operator, this is Miss Lynn and I'm calling in an emergency. Connect me with the airport."

No, no, no. This cannot be happening. Kathy's going to think I have brought her to Loonyville.

"I want to report a UFO sighting. Well, I didn't really see it but I heard it…Because I know what a UFO sounds like, I saw and heard one in Florida…What do you mean what do I want you to do? I want you to send planes up there to catch it." Our silence was broken as she slid the screen door open to return to the deck.

"Mom, we have to be going. Kathy really has to get ready for school tomorrow."

The ride to drop Kathy off at her parents' home was deafeningly quiet except for the car's engine and the sound of other UFO's whizzing overhead on their way to landing at the airport. When we arrived at her parents' house, neither of us spoke as we continued to sit in the driveway. Finally, I turned to this woman, who up until about a half-hour earlier I pictured as my future wife, and the only words that made it from my heart to my mouth were: "Kathy, I'm so sorry."

Kathy took both of my hands, looked into my eyes and gently said, "I'm going out with Andrew Joseph, not Andrew Joseph's mom." We kissed and never mentioned the UFO encounter ever again…except for the dozens of times during our lengthy marriage when Kathy reminds me of my UFO genetic stock.

That summer Kathy and I became engaged. As Kathy and I grew closer and closer, Mom and Len were growing further and further apart. It was difficult for Mom to accept the fact that I was entering a new phase of my life. Not just her son, I was going to be Kathy's husband, as well.

When Len contemplated resigning from his social organization, I warned him for the sake of their marriage not to do it. His idea was that resigning to work in Mom's GANBC travel business, would rekindle the flame of their marriage. I knew from personal experience growing up that being with Mom 24/7/365 is dangerous for one's own sanity. Almost on a nightly basis we would have driveway chats about his pending resignation. At the same time Mom would encourage him to resign so that they could run the business together (or more factually, so he could be her errand boy). Len resigned, and their marriage continued to unravel.

The Blizzard of '78 dropped four to six feet of snow on Rhode Island. It started on a Monday, February 6th, and snowed continuously for days. It wasn't until Friday that most of the main streets were plowed enough for two cars to be able to barely squeeze by.

On Friday, I heard shoveling outside in our yard, but looking out the windows all I could see were huge drifts of snow, some cresting as high as eight or ten feet. Using the inside stairway, I went to the main entrance and the front door to find out who was out shoveling the driveway. Mom spotted me and said Len had insisted on shoveling a path down the driveway out to the street.

After winterizing myself to look like the abominable snowman, I joined Len outside the main front door. He had made little progress even though he had been out in the nightmarish winter wonderland for a half-hour. I asked him what was going on, since our snowplow guy had called to say he would not be up to our house until Sunday at the earliest.

"Your mother's insane. She's having a poker game this afternoon and I have to clear a path to the street."

One or two nights every week, Mom would set up two – sometimes three - large poker tables in the main foyer and fill them with poker fanatics like her. Len once told me she represented the "house" and would skim 10% off every pot from each table. In return she would host the game and spring for the ladies' drinks, food and dessert goodies. Not a bad revenue stream, albeit a tad illegal.

"Len, you mean to tell me, we have to shovel a seventy foot pathway down to the street for my mother's poker game? How does she expect them to get up the hill?"

"You don't know these women very well, Andy. Snow and icy conditions mean nothing. They'll crawl over glass to play cards."

Hours later we finished tunneling a small path through the snow just in time to see cars dropping off their female passengers, some lugging their favorite, lucky folding chairs. As I walked back to the house and through the main entrance, the ladies, mostly hefty, were already noshing. My mom saw Len with his frozen eyebrows and me with my frozen beard and commented, 'Ladies, a special round of applause for my husband and son who made our game possible by clearing the snow so you could be here."

I looked at Len and he at me. Guaranteed the same thought simultaneously went through both of our minds. Who was going to get to push Mom into the crackling fire raging in the fireplace?

I went upstairs, showered, dressed in another dry abominable snowman outfit, and walked down the side stairway. Listening to the cackling ladies giving the cackling fire a run for its money, I left the house.

Approximately three hours later, on foot, I finally finished my freedom trail trek to Kathy's parents' house.

Shortly after the blizzard, I decided that with our approaching wedding three months away, I should send out a resume seeking a position within the advertising field. A month later, I was hired as an advertising manager with a New Jersey based international company. This enraged my mother, who had already decided that Kathy and I would marry and move into The Big House and live happily ever after with her and Len, and never mind that their marriage was tanking.

A couple of months before my New Jersey start date, my relationship with Mom grew more and more antagonistic. Len met me one morning as I was heading for my car to relay a message from Mom: "Andy, your mother wanted me to tell you that she would appreciate your making less noise coming up the back stairs to your apartment at all hours of the night."

"Well, Len, I would suggest you advise your wife that her son said if she has anything to say about when he comes or when he goes, she should have the gumption to tell him this face-to-face and not through you."

As I opened my apartment door a few days after Len delivered my return message to Mom, I found a note from her ordering me to vacate my apartment immediately, as she rented it that very afternoon. I flew down the two flights of stairs, passing through the outer office and into hers. I flung her note on the desk and asked her what was going on. She informed me that she now had to worry about herself since I was moving to New Jersey, and she had the opportunity to rent the studio apartment to a fine gentleman. After reminding her that I co-owned the property and had no intention of moving out, I left.

Needless to say, there was no "fine gentleman," just one more vindictive "I'll show you for moving away" scheme. Over the remaining weeks prior to my New Jersey relocation, other notes followed. I would toss them in the wastebasket without reading them. One time Mom heard me coming down my back stairway and opened the hall door to confront me over not responding to her notes. She became livid when I told her I was not interested in reading anything she wrote, preferring to wait for the movie.

Dealing with a major out-of-state relocation is one thing, dealing with a delusional Miss Lynn who viewed herself as the loving matriarch of a happy family was another. Thank God dealing with Kathy and our plans for our wedding, less than four weeks away, was a welcomed distraction from move-related pressures and the stress of dealing with Mom.

8. Our Wedding

Before I accepted the New Jersey position, I made sure the company was aware that my start date was less than two weeks before my wedding and honeymoon. They were very accommodating, certain that two weeks would be enough time for me to get acclimated. The company made arrangements for me to stay at a hotel near their headquarters. All expenses would be paid until Kathy and I found housing.

Here comes the bride all dressed in white...

Whatever the eventual outcome of the marriage, most every bride looks back at her wedding as a frenzied, fun and positively memorable day. Kathy had a different experience.

Yes, she enjoyed the crazed chaos of the final hours with her mom and bridesmaids before our 6PM church ceremony. So much so, it appeared, that she was a few minutes late arriving at the church (leaving a very nervous groom pacing in the room off the altar at St. Mary's Church for what seemed hours...little did I know that this tardiness would be my wife's MO throughout the next three plus decades). And yes, the moment I finally spotted my beautiful Kathy at the back of the church, a vision in a magnificent while gown, veil covering her glowing face and shimmering hair, I knew I was experiencing a moment I would remember forever.

And then, without warning Miss Lynn suddenly appeared next to my bride, wearing her own white gown. It had been previously agreed upon that the mothers – Kathy's mom, my stepmother Val, and Miss Lynn – would wear light blue to coordinate with the color scheme Kathy had selected for *her* wedding. Right beside Mom stood Len, also wearing a white suit instead of the dark brown suit the fathers had agreed upon.

The groomsmen were already lined up ready to process on the traditional white runner that had been rolled down the aisle. Our friend (and the music director at St. Mary's Church) was just about to play the traditional wedding march when:

Not so fast! Stop everything! Miss Lynn is in the house, er, church.

One of the groomsmen was obliged to step out of formation to escort Miss Lynn and Len down the aisle on the pristine white runner intended for the bride and her attendants, and once again

Miss Lynn managed to upstage everyone – including the bride - in order to make her grand entrance. What, no tiara?

After they were escorted down the aisle, she and Len were led to the second pew on the groom's side. Since she was not at the church when the other parents arrived and were seated (and there was always a chance that Mom would be a no-show), Dad and Val were occupying the first pew. I, and half of the church, heard my mother yelp: "They're in my seat! I want them removed from my seat!"

If looks could kill, Miss Lynn *all dressed in white* would have been vaporized by me on the spot.

With all eyes now off the bride and focused on the ruckus going on at the front of the church, Miss Lynn was in her glory. Dad and Val quietly moved to the number two pew in order for Miss Lynn to be number one.

My best man, leaned in my direction and said, "In an hour she'll be out of your life."

Glancing over at my mother, I said, "No, Jack, in an hour she'll be in my life and in Kathy's life, as well."

As I stared at her, the smirk on her face said it all: I won, I won!

The organ started to play and all eyes turned to see beautiful Kathy, the events of the past few minutes were all but forgotten with the first notes of "Here Comes the Bride."

Father Wilfred Hept, a Franciscan priest and my friend of many years, performed the ceremony. Given our late start, I expected he would compensate by moving things along. I knew we were in trouble when he said that the bride and groom should take a seat for his sermon. After his personal and interminable homily I whispered to Kathy, "He pretty much covered everything in the Bible, except maybe the locusts."

Kathy's two brothers were both participants in our wedding - Bob assisted Father Wilfred on the altar and Joe was a groomsman - so neither of them was sitting with their families during the ceremony. From time to time we would hear the pitter-patter of little feet (in the quiet church it sounded more like the running of the bulls) and daddy-can't- get-me giggles. Since Joe was sitting in the pew with the other groomsmen, I couldn't see him, but up on the altar my soon to be brother-in-law, Bob, gave his clip-clopping three year old son, John, a look so intimidating I wanted to shout: "I'm sorry, I'm sorry!"

When the anticipated forty-five minute mass and marriage ceremony concluded after an hour and a half, we decided in light of the darkening dusk to skip the scheduled pictures at Roger Williams Park and go directly to the reception. Unfortunately, the second limo didn't get the message and headed straight to the park.

En route to our reception, Kathy quietly said to me, "Your mom is some piece of work."

I joked, "Kathy, it's only the beginning for us. I've had 27 years of it so far. Glad I can now share her with you." Little did we realize how prophetic those words would turn out to be.

As soon as we arrived at Metacomet Country Club for our reception, we realized that the other limo, carrying half of the wedding party, was nowhere in sight. This being 1978, we had no way to contact them and had to hope they'd catch up with us sooner rather than later.

The wedding planner guided us to the bar off the reception room with members of (half) the wedding party. Here we could take a breath before greeting family and friends in the receiving line. In addition to the bartender setting up his bar, there was an older gentleman nearby, who came over to give Kathy a hug and shake my hand. It was Kathy's Uncle Pete. As we stood talking Miss Lynn stormed into the room.

"Do you people realize it's after 8 and these people are hungry?"

We were all aware of the time. My stomach was in knots of anxiety while we waited to hear from the rest of our wedding party.

"If you don't do something right away, they're going to leave."

My only response: "We'll see if we can get doggie bags for them." She stomped out of the room.

Uncle Pete, who had seen my mother in action earlier at the church, was suddenly standing in front of me with two glasses of gin and tonic. "Here, drink these. I think you're going to need them."

After ten or fifteen more agonizing minutes the other limo finally arrived to drop off the rest of our group.

The planner hurriedly lined us up. The doors were opened and just as quickly, abruptly shut again. Miss Lynn did not like the composition of the receiving line. Traditionally the bride's mom and dad are the first to greet the guests flanked by the bride and groom, and followed by the groom's mom and dad. Because of the divorce, my mom and Len came after me and were followed by my Dad and Val.

What was Mom's beef? She did not want to stand next to Big Andrew and Val.

So much for her concern for the waiting, starving guests.

If it had been up to me, I would have waited it out until our time for the reception expired. Phyllis, my new mother-in-law, graciously interceded and suggested that my Here-comes-Miss Lynn-all-dressed-in-white mother and Len be first in line to greet everyone, while she and my father-in-law moved to second place.

In retrospect it seems weirdly appropriate for Miss Lynn and Len to be the first in line, since they had the most experience. Together they had a combined 8 marriages between them. Another marriage or two would follow for Len after he and Miss Lynn were eventually split asunder.

Long before our wedding, Kathy and I agreed that since we were paying for the wedding we would set a cap of one hundred combined guests for our parents to invite: Fifty for Kathy's parents and twenty-five each for my divorced parents. If any parent exceeded their allotment, they would have to pay only the cost of the meal for any additional guests. In a hate-filled letter to her unappreciative son and ungrateful daughter-in-law written many years after our wedding reception, mom "reminded" us that she and Len had paid for an open bar the entire evening. This was news to both of us, since we paid for an hour of open bar with our guests paying for their own drinks after that.

Did any parent exceed their guest quota? Yes. Did each of them pay the meal cost for their additions? Yes.

After all our guests were welcomed, we were two hours behind schedule. Our guests were still famished after the hors d'oeuvres, so we arranged for dinner to be served while the wedding party was photographed in the foyer.

The photographer had just started taking various shots when the door from the dining room to the foyer blew open and dear old tempestuous Mom cycloned in and demanded to speak to me. I stepped over to her with an icy, "What?"

"I want to talk to you privately. This is an emergency."

Lifting my ring finger sporting its bright new wedding band, I recall saying, "Privately ended about two hours ago. What's your emergency?"

"Well, I noticed that *the other end* has some tables in the front area and some of my guests are stuck at the back tables. I want everyone I invited at the front tables and move all of your father's side to the back." The six gin and tonics supplied to me by my now favorite Uncle Pete took control as I bluntly said to Mom: "Your choice. Return to your seat or your car. Either way won't make a difference to me."

She left. Picture taking resumed as did the rest of our evening.

Throughout dinner, neither Lynn nor Len touched a morsel of food. What, and miss an opportunity to perform before a captive audience? No way! Instead they took to the empty dance floor and entertained our guests by showing off their latest Arthur Murray Dance Studio moves. I was amazed neither of them complained to me about not having a follow spot.

Later that night after arriving at our hotel, Kathy and I wondered half-seriously if we'd actually been married at some point during all of the hoopla. After thirty-five years, four grown children and two well-behaved dogs (make that one well-behaved dog and one yellow lab); I can testify that we did, in fact, get married on May 26, 1978.

As our wedding gift, Mom gave us a honeymoon package including air, hotel and meals. At first it was a great honeymoon until I realized what was really going on. I didn't tell Kathy (Note to Kathy: Surprise!) but this "gift" was not from Mom. Our entire honeymoon package – including air transportation - was given to us by the hotel and was known as a "fam" (familiarization) trip provided absolutely free by the hotel property to familiarize a tour operator (me) with their facilities, including their restaurants, in exchange for the opportunity of snagging future group tour business. Well, at least that explained the frequent interruptions by the hotel sales department.

Arriving back at New York's Kennedy Airport, we newlyweds split up. Kathy left to board a Rhode Island bound plane, and I went to our parked car to head to New Jersey.

Sensing how lonely it must be for me, on a daily basis when the company mail was delivered, I would receive inspiring notes and cards from my mother-in-law. During this same period, I was also receiving notes from Mom containing messages like, "Someday people will leave you high and dry just like you left your mother high and dry."

Knowing that I was always in my office early every morning, my mother-in-law would convince the overnight switchboard operators to put her calls through to surprise me. Mom also called: To complain about Len, her office crew, the difficulty of running GANBC and, did I mention Len?

If I was out of the office, my secretary would be the recipient of Miss Lynn's ire over her inability to locate or interrupt me. When I got back to my office, in with various pink message slips would be one checked URGENT with a note: "Miss Lynn requires a return call. It's an emergency." Another argument with Len? Did Alice show up late for work this morning? Was Frisky, the cat, out all night?

On weekends Kathy would fly to New Jersey and we would go house hunting. During Kathy's last weekend visit we found a wonderful condo in South Jersey, which we could rent with an option to buy. There were a number of communities nearby where Kathy could pursue her teaching career. The only drawback was the two hour daily commute for me: one hour up to Northern Jersey and one hour home. In drive-time traffic these commutes could double.

On Monday I discussed this with a few guys at work; two of them were already car-pooling each day from that area and thought it would be great adding a third.

On Thursday of that same week, I had the uncomfortable assignment of giving the company's long time advertising agency a ninety-day notice that we would be severing ties with them by moving all advertising in-house under my leadership. We had lunch in New York, but before I could mention the reason for the meeting, the agency execs conducted me on a brief walk down memory lane. Their agency and my company had had many experiences together, including some ugly, borderline – and to my mind - criminal behavior. I never did tell the ad execs I was there to fire them.

When I returned to the office, I met with the company's executive vice president, who confirmed what I had just heard and encouraged me to visit QC. I dropped by the quality control department, and they candidly added more details to what the exec VP had just told me. How the hell was this possible? We have a federal government inspection office on the premises staffed by a U.S. agent.

I was informed that the agent was only on the premises one day a week, and on that day most production would be moved to another shift, leaving only a couple of lines open and running at an extremely lowered speed thereby guaranteeing we would pass government standards when samples were pulled during their runs. Back in my office I found an article on my desk. It dealt with an amusement park's roller-coaster ride seizing up. A typed, unsigned note accompanying the article, mentioned a link between our company's product and a recent house fire. After what I'd learned during my New York meeting, these incidents seemed not only possible, but highly probable.

After a sleepless night I left the hotel around 4AM to drive to Rhode Island. I called Kathy to meet me for a quick breakfast before she left for her last day of school. Over breakfast I told her what I'd found out the day before and said there was no way I could work there and promote their products. Kathy agreed and said she would hold off her plan to submit her resignation at the end of the school day.

Next stop was visiting Mom to tell her about my decision and notify her that Kathy and I would be occupying the studio apartment until we could find our own place. Mom insisted we move into the five room second floor apartment, which had been completed while I was away. This carved up the main two floors of living space into two separate residences. I later found out she had already rented the studio apartment to the son of one of her card playing regulars.

9. Return to The Big House

After our move to The Big House, Kathy and I settled in our temporary digs while searching for our own place.

Mom and I came to an agreement that I would assist her with GANBC's marketing in exchange for the downstairs office staff answering my phone lines, as I would be reopening my marketing and advertising business in the third floor office. Luckily, I had not resigned from my previous accounts prior to my move to Jersey as I intended to continue handling them on a long distance basis. Now, I had a base of business to build upon.

One of the first knock down battles between Mom and me occurred over my persistent insistence that the company be rebranded with a new name. Since no one knew what the acronym GANBC stood for and only a very few could pronounce it, I sought an easy to recall name without linking it to a past involving the beauty industry. I selected the name "Great Age" which was to reflect retirement (and pre-retirement) years as being a time period for one to look forward to, a Great Age.

Predictably these meetings would result in a shouting match ending with one of us exiting without any resolution. One time Mom stated, "I built the GANBC business over the past five years to where it is today. It had nothing to do with your so-called marketing skills."

As I left I remarked, "Yes, you built it to operate out of the basement office of a house where it will remain for the next 25 years or until it's forced to shut down."

These shouting matches were not confined to the offices. They also erupted between Lynn and Len who were living on the first floor. Worst were the times she would deliberately provoke him by calling him "little boy". Len would then resort to screaming right back, retaliating with a personal put-down he could call his own. For our own sanity, Kathy and I would leave the war zone and visit friends or family.

The beginning of July we were elated to find an apartment close to my office yet far enough away from Lynn and Len's verbal brawls. We would not be able to move in until the apartment remodeling was finished toward the end of August. Surely we could endure the balance of the summer living in The Big House.

We dropped by to tell Mom and Len we had found an apartment and signed a lease to move in on September 1st. To Kathy they appeared happy for us. However, I knew my mother; behind the insincere smile something was brewing.

A week later the something arrived, a note slipped under our door stating, "You people will have to move your things out of the second floor apartment. I leased it yesterday and he's moving in August 1st. You two can live in one of the rooms in your office upstairs; it'll only be for a month."

My mind was spinning. I had become use to living my life with a spiteful, avenging mother pulling the rug out from under me whenever (no car on prom night), but now she was spreading her spite to another target, my innocent wife, which made me spitting mad.

Mom knew exactly what she was doing. She wanted us to suffer because we were moving out, moving on. What better way to put the screws to us than forcing us to live where there was no access to a bathroom or a kitchen?

I thought the best way to tell Kathy of our move upstairs was to take her to lunch away from the *mad* house. Kathy came from an extremely stable and loving family, a family with a mother who would literally kill for her young as opposed to mine, who would seriously consider killing her young if she couldn't control him.

Never having met a person like my mother before, Kathy wondered if Mom had been this way all of her life. I told her that from what I'd been told and through my own experience, Mom had always been a manipulative, vindictive, lying user; at times completely disconnected from reality and unable to sustain personal relationships. That said, any other questions about Mom?

Kathy quipped, "I'm thinking of the better or worse thing we agreed to a couple of months ago, is this the worse?"

"Kathy, we're talking Miss Lynn here. You ain't seen nothin' yet. She's the gift that keeps on giving."

Our future landlord was very accommodating and agreed to allow us to store our furniture in the completed bedrooms in the apartment until we moved in.

Living without a kitchen did not prove to be a major issue. We usually ate breakfast and lunch out. Dinner invitations flowed in when relatives and friends learned of our plight. Len would stop by my office and offer to grill dinner for us. I appreciated his efforts but declined. Once when Kathy and I were leaving to go to a friend's house for dinner, Mom called from the pool that "you people" are welcome to join them for dinner. I passed.

Part of our nightly dine-out with family and friends, and probably the highlight, was being able to take a shower before heading home to our campsite, my office. There was a sink and working commode in the outdoor pool's cabana. If nature called during the night for either of us, we'd have to walk down three flights of stairs and outdoors. Once outside, we would walk around the darkened house to use the even darker cabana. Add some rain to the mix, and you'd have two rather unhappy (and damp) mattress-on-the-floor campers.

Len was more than aware of our wee hour treks to the cabana and offered to leave the back door to their residence unlocked in order for us to use the bathroom in their place (right off their bedroom, yeah, right) or the office lavatory in the basement. I appreciated the offer but for obvious reasons declined.

When Kathy and I returned from lunch one afternoon, we stopped by the lower office to pick-up my messages. I noticed there were some people there to book trips, when Miss Lynn tripped into the office barefooted and with a towel wrapped around her dripping bathing suit. This was not unusual. A good chunk of Miss Lynn's summertime office hours were spent either in the pool or slathering on oil to get a tan. What was unusual this time was that after Mom returned to her pool activities, I overheard a comment made by one of the ladies there to book a tour. "Miss Lynn has more oil on her than a Purdue chicken."

During this period arguments on the first floor grew in intensity, loudness and frequency. Len would vent by telling me how impossible my mother was, and I would say: "Deal with her for 27 years as I've done and then come talk to me."

Len got a respite (of a sort) every Thursday when he headed to Mattapoisett, Massachusetts, to visit his elderly mother and take her shopping and to doctor appointments. He would usually arrive back home on Friday afternoons to face Miss Lynn and whatever mood she would be in to greet him.

You cannot believe how ecstatic we were when the phone rang

with the news, "The movers are here!" Our apartment was finished on August 22nd and we moved in on the 24th. The first thing we did once we got there was hug our new toilet, sink and shower before heading to the kitchen to embrace the refrigerator and stove. The movers must have thought us certifiable. We didn't care. If they only knew the crazoid conditions we'd endured over the past month, they would probably have joined us in our appliance hugging.

A sense of normalcy entered our lives: We would enjoy a quick breakfast together before Kathy would head to school and I to my office up at The Big House, being extra careful to avoid my mother.

Soon after we moved out, Miss Lynn discarded her vengeful Mom persona and became a sorrowful mother whose only child had abandoned her. Of course it never occurred to her that showing our apartment at The Big House and renting it out without our knowledge, and then slipping an eviction note under our door might have had a little something to do with it. Not to mention the outdoor facilities three floors down and around the house by the pool. And the fact that I was an equal owner in the property!

The sorrowful Mom routine did not play well to the office staff or Len. Eyes would roll when the curtain rose on her crocodile-teared performances. I had witnessed this all of my life; it was part of my Mom's MO; drive people away and then blame them for leaving.

No sooner would Mom be off to escort a tour when Len would leave for days, presumably spending time helping his mom. Since all calls requiring their attention would be forwarded to me, I couldn't help knowing how long he was away. Managing their business was a distraction; the more time I had to spend on GANBC, the less time I could spend on my own.

While they were both away in early December (he visiting his mom and she out on tour) a Montreal hotel called wanting to know if GANBC was going to use its room block of 50 rooms (usually a one bus movement would require 25 rooms, two buses 50 rooms) over the peak New Year's holiday. I placed the call on hold and checked our counts: One bus was sold out and the other only had 6 people booked on it. The hotel caller was instructed to release 25 rooms of the 50 room block.

Mom arrived back from her multi-day tour late in the afternoon and literally bounded up the three flights of stairs, sputtering all the way.

Here's the gist of our tete-a-tete:

MOM *(incensed)*: You canceled my rooms in Montreal for New Year's?

ME: I cut the room block from 50 to 25 to accommodate the full bus already sold. It was dumb to keep a bus open with only 6 passengers at this late date. People who want to travel for New Year's have already made plans which do not include traveling with GANBC.

MOM: You were not authorized to do this. You call the hotel back right now and get those rooms back.

ME: If you want the rooms back, you call them.

MOM: I'm not calling them but I'll show you, you call the six passengers to tell them you canceled their trips.

ME: The six passengers have already been moved to a Paragon Tour which was priced $40 per passenger higher than GANBC's. Deducting Paragon's commission to you, the cost to GANBC is only $16 per passenger. Under a hundred bucks total as opposed to your taking a bath of over four thousand dollars in empty rooms and empty bus seats.

MOM: That's not the point.

ME: What is the point?

MOM: The point is you made a decision without consulting me.

ME *(going back to my work)* You're welcome.

I was told that she was still babbling when she got down to the basement office and screamed at the staff that they had no right to transfer the call up to me. GANBC was her business and only she was able to make decisions and if anyone did not want to follow her rules, they should leave. Intimidating the office crew because an irate hotel was calling for the final rooming list 30 days before a prime arrival date, like New Year's Eve? Not cool. Carrying on in front of the people in your office charged with selling future tours?

Inexcusable.

Something told me the Miss Lynn scourge would not be limited to the office folks and me. There was plenty left over awaiting Len's arrival back home later that night. Sure enough, Len appeared at The Big House around 8PM. By 8:30, Len had left the building, the business and the marriage.

The next morning a genuinely tearful, or so I thought, mother came up to my office as soon as I got in to tell me her side of the story concluding with, "I want a divorce and have a call in to Attorney *Incompetent*."

"For the love of God," I said, "Would you face reality for once in your life? Your attorney botched up one of your corporation filings. He's an imbecile. You need a high powered divorce law firm. You know Len is buddy-buddy with one of the executive partners at *Huge Law Firm*."

After making a few calls I was able to secure a meeting with a top divorce attorney at one of the best known RI divorce law firms, Kirshenbaum & Kirshenbaum. He agreed to a meeting with Mom and me that afternoon.

Happy that I was able to set up a meeting with such short notice, I went down to Mom's office to share the news. As soon as I walked in I, and the entire office including those making reservations, could hear her screeching in her office through two closed doors.

Turns out, Len's attorney was already calling her with a cash demand to have Len not return to the premises. I asked her for the phone and informed him of our meeting that afternoon with an attorney who would be representing my mother. As soon as I gave him this info, I hung the phone up, cutting off Mom's howls at Len's attorney, who up until that point had been a friend to them both.

When we met with her potential attorney that afternoon, I presented the financial facts of their relationship in order for him to have a full understanding of the background finances of who put what into the marriage. It was important to protect her stock position since she was a 50% shareholder in GANBC Realty Corp., owner of The Big House. It was too much for Mom to sit there and listen, and she soon began bombarding her new attorney with demands, number one being that Len wasn't getting a dime from her. The meeting was productive but surreal. The best way I could describe it was the attorney and I were conversing in English while Mom was speaking in Swahili.

The lawyer instructed Mom to make a list of all their joint assets as well as her personal assets. She remained stuck on the, "Everything is mine, he gets nothing since he walked out of the marriage" track as I ushered her out of his office, promising him the list by the following day.

I followed my mother back to her office and attempted to gather the information her attorney required. While I tried to compile the assets and separate what was theirs, his or hers, she continued to spout about how she would show him and take him for everything he is worth. I reminded her of the extent of his possessions: his clothes and his elderly mother. Therefore she had vastly more to lose than he did; it would be in her best interest to comply with her lawyer's request.

After the locksmith had changed all the locks in the house and office, I left feeling as though I had been wrought dry in a wringer. Before I left, Mom assured me she would have the information for the lawyer by the morning.

The next morning Mom handed over the completed asset documents. After making a few corrections, I compiled all of the information into a spreadsheet and had it delivered to her attorney. Later that afternoon, I received a call from her attorney, who said he had spoken to Len's attorney and they were attempting to establish an amount Mom would have to pay to Len in order to keep him from returning to their "happy home". He asked me to convey this to Mom, as he was in no mood to hear her shrieking at him.

I called Mom's extension and told her I would meet her on the first floor to discuss my conversation with her attorney. As I was going down the stairs I thought, HE was in no mood to hear her, what made him think I was?

Mom had both guns blazing when I got there. "What right does my attorney have talking to you about my case?" I attempted to explain that based on her demeanor in his office the previous afternoon, he thought it best I speak with you. This approach proved futile and only elevated her anger. Now she was furious with her new attorney for breaching client confidentiality and swore she was going to fix him and have him disbarred. I countered: his disbarment wasn't the issue, her screwing up her third marriage was.

As I got up to leave, I reminded her that the only person who remained loyal to her, helping her and bailing her out no matter what was me. But I, like everyone else in her life, was now ready to throw in the towel.

She asked me to sit down and discuss what had to be done. I explained that we had to first get the wolf away from the door (my favorite expression, in case you haven't noticed), and Len was the wolf. Because there was no pre-nuptial agreement, we would have to minimize the loss to GANBC and her GANBC Realty stock. At this stage in our discussion Mom was whimpering while I tried to be as objective and emotionless as possible.

The next morning Mom's attorney called to present their outrageous cash demand to cover Len's expenses while he waited a few months for the preliminary divorce hearing. I told him to relay our best offer of $10,000. He called back with their final offer of $25,000. "In that case, please tell Len's attorney – and Len – that Mom withdraws the offer and is willing to welcome her husband back to her loving arms. It might, however, be a good idea for him to wear some sort of battle gear.

A short time later Mom's attorney called back and said they would accept $10,000 plus a mounted antique whaling harpoon. I said we would have a check delivered to him for that amount, but I would have to search for the harpoon as I had never seen it.

When I met with Mom to tell her the news, she took it much better than I expected, only remarking that the harpoon in question was under their bed. She wondered why he wanted that old thing. I told her either he was considering a career change to become a whaler or he was afraid of her and wanted to protect himself.

While waiting for the preliminary hearing date, all was quiet. Once the date was set, I am sure Len was prepped by his attorney at least as well as Mom's attorney attempted to prep her. Can you say how do you hold a tiger by the tail?

The day of the hearing, Kathy and I sat in the courtroom, which overlooked a hillside where a row of cars were parked, including Len's. Mom as the plaintiff was first to testify. Instead of factually answering her lawyer's questions, she would veer off topic to lob personal attacks at Len. When Len's attorney began his questioning, it went pretty much as I expected. She immediately started jabbing at him for representing Len while being a mutual friend to them both.

Earlier on, I had hired a private investigator to come to the courtroom. On cue as soon as Len got up on the witness stand, he left the courtroom. From our vantage point near the window, Kathy and I watched while our investigator guided a tow truck driver to Len's car before hitching it up and towing it away.

Perfectly legal. The vehicle was owned by and registered to GANBC.

After both attorneys rested the judge said he would issue a ruling whether or not the case would proceed to divorce court. While Mom wanted to stick around to admonish her attorney some more for not asking her the *right* questions, I grabbed her arm and rushed her to our car in the parking lot.

Kathy and I let her blather on about her incompetent attorney all the way back to the house. When we got there, I opened the side door to enter the carriage house and flipped the light switch to reveal Len's car. Inside the ignition was the spare set of keys I had given the investigator. I told Mom and Kathy to go through everything in the car including the glove compartment while I checked the trunk.

Jackpot.

A box of letters and a bag full of credit card receipts for gas, restaurants and New Hampshire motels were scooped up and carried into the house.

All the letters were from the same woman. Each of them referenced their love for each other and described their body parts in explicit detail. A good number of them referred to their illicit meeting of the previous night, which tied in nicely with the various motel receipts.

So much for helping out dear, elderly, frail mom on Thursdays. Len might have been stopping by his mom's – maybe to pick up more letters mailed to him at her address - but I doubt he was spending much time ferrying her around. The receipts showed that before too long Len was on his way to New Hampshire for his regular afternoon – and evening – delights.

Kathy and I gathered all of the letters and receipts. I told my mother to not answer her phone, because her lawyer would probably be calling to have the car returned to Len. I had already taken the registration out of the car. I told Mom in the event the police came looking for "Len's" car, she should produce the registration to show it is owned by GANBC. Kathy and I found an instant copy center still open and made multiple copies of everything in the trunk, just in case.

The next morning after Mom had a night to stew over her unfaithful mate, she had a list of demands before she would turn the car back over to Len: she wanted the ten thousand dollars back along with "that damn spear" plus a formal letter from Len confessing to his sexual exploits.

"Absolutely not," I said. Len could have his car back as long as he re-registered it under his own name, and he also had to have proof of insurance. This would relieve GANBC of any liability. After arguing about this for most of the morning (she determined to nail her two timing spouse, me wanting to put the whole thing in the rear view mirror), Mom finally gave in.

Monday morning Len was able to retrieve his car with everything intact. Ah, everything except the letters and receipts.

As if the weird could not get weirder, Mom's divorce attorney quietly dropped her case. This after being provided with proof of her husband's yearlong infidelity. A guaranteed sure-fire win. Mom swore she hadn't annoyed him with calls making new demands in light of the new evidence. Yet something told me otherwise.

The hunt was on for another attorney to pick up the pieces of the case. I received a few suggestions from friends. One of those recommended to me was known for his outlandishly outrageous courtroom antics: Aram Barbarian. His behavior before the court was notorious and he was unabashed at pointing out flaws in the legal system. He once brought a hand grenade into a courtroom to illustrate how ineffective a new (and expensive) weapon screening device was. When I asked him about this, his allegorical response was, "Who else is there to tell the emperor he isn't wearing any clothes?"

During our meeting with Aram, I went over the facts, seeking protection of business and real estate assets. Mom on the other hand, wanted to page through the love letters and read the juiciest parts. Aram could not have been more disinterested and attempted to interrupt her several times to express his desire to end the meeting.

When the actual case was heard, Aram called Mom to the stand and did not let her wander from the main theme: Len left the marriage relationship. He did this without a murmur about there being letters proving an affair.

Frustrated, Mom turned obnoxious and surly when cross-examined by Len's attorney, injecting the existence of letters and motel receipts to almost every question he asked her. If he had asked her if it was a sunny day outside, she would have said, "As a matter of fact it is sunny. A perfect day to sit outside and read the sexually explicit love letters sent to my husband by his mistress."

When it came time for each attorney to deliver his closing argument, Aram stood up and delivered these words: "Your honor, Mr. and Mrs. Simmons were living in a marital relationship. Suddenly Mr. Simmons decides to leave and wants Mrs. Simmons to pay. It's like when we were kids and played baseball. If I decided to leave and take my ball and bat to play in another game thereby ending this game, does that entitle me to your glove as well?" Aram sat down with copies of all of the love letters and receipts on the table in front of him. None had been introduced into evidence.

From our seats directly in back of Mom and Aram, it was obvious to Kathy and me that Mom was exasperated with Aram for not sharing Len's infidelity with the world or at least the courtroom.

I could see her agitation building as Len's lawyer detailed their assets, including the business and real estate. Unable to understand that what she was hearing was what any divorce attorney would be saying on behalf of his client, Mom took each statement personally and kept nudging Aram to interrupt in protest.

After both sides rested the judge left the courtroom to consider his decision. The lawyers went to the back of the courtroom to talk shop or the latest barrister gossip. Mom remained at her table, leafing through the letters, occasionally murmuring out loud, "This is so disgusting" or "What a pig" or some other noxious phrase.

Mom's feigned disgust was an effort to engage Len into arguing with her. It made no apparent impression on him though, as he quietly sat at the opposite table. Once Mom caught sight of the two lawyers chatting in light-hearted conversation at the back of the courtroom, she said to us, "Look at them. No wonder why Aram didn't fight hard enough for me. They're friends." I quietly told her all lawyers are friends outside the courtroom.

The judge returned and the court was called to order. He granted the divorce to Mom and the only asset awarded to Len was his beloved whaling harpoon.

After Aram packed his papers into his briefcase and Mom packed hers with the letters and receipts, we went into the hall. I thanked Aram for what he had done for Mom. She on the other hand was not so thankful, demanding to know why he hadn't entered the letters and receipts into evidence.

Aram paused and looked at me before speaking, "Would you kindly explain to Mrs. Simmons what I just did in there for her? Good day." He walked away, and Kathy and I quickly escorted Mom to the elevator to avoid her desired confrontation with Len.

On our way home, Mom suggested we stop for a celebratory lunch. While we were eating Mom started to cry, because now she was all alone in The Big House. The second floor tenant had long since moved out along with the person renting the studio apartment.

Mom would later come up with a completely different story. According to her recollection, it all began the night she and Len, along with Kathy's parents, were having dinner at our new apartment, and they all noticed the curtains swaying in a winter draft. It was then that Mom and Len magnanimously offered us the second floor apartment even if it meant forcing their current tenants to move.

A few problems with this dippy theory. In the first place, Len was long gone. Secondly, Kathy's parents viewed my mother as insincere and avoided her company. And third, the second floor tenants, who had moved in the previous August 1st and displaced Kathy and me, had broken their lease and vacated the apartment mid-November months before this celebratory spring lunch.

Kathy and I discussed it at length before we decided to move back. We knew there would be irritants, and there were, like the way Mom would leave her wet washed clothes in the washer for Kathy to dry and fold before doing ours; or the way she would call up the front stairs from her place to yell up some tidbit of urgent –

in her mind – news any hour of the day…or night.

Speaking of the stairway, Mom was adamant that we not install any kind of lock on our side of the door leading down her stairs, although she had a lock on her side. One day my mother-in-law and Kathy's cousin, Barbara, were visiting a very pregnant Kathy. Apparently, Mom had forgotten to lock the door on her side and when my mother-in-law leaned against it, it swung open and she started to topple. If it hadn't been for Kathy's cousin, who grabbed her arm, she would have fallen down a full flight of stairs.

Despite my mother's fury, "You have no right doing that," I immediately put a lock on our side of the door. All I could think about was Kathy or our soon-to-be born first child having a similar accident. Not on my watch.

The studio apartment was eventually rented to a friend of ours, a quiet young woman known to us both for years.

All in all, life was good. My business was doing well. With the divorce behind her, Mom concentrated on GANBC.

Then the phone call came in that changed our lives.

10. Canary in a Coal Mine

On a Friday afternoon, sometime after 5, our house phone rang.   It was Janet, who worked for Mom, calling from the downstairs office to tell me there was an emergency telephone call. On my way down to the office I wondered if it had anything to do with Mom who was escorting one of her groups to the Canary Islands.

The upset caller was from the accounting department of the tour operator from which Mom had purchased her Canary Islands tour packages. He informed me that GANBC's check paying for the trips had been returned to them due to insufficient funds, adding unless we wired the money to their office by Monday morning, Mom and her passengers would not be allowed to board their returning flight on Wednesday thereby stranding them. With deepest apologies, I assured him we would wire the funds to them on Monday morning and asked that he contact me once the funds were received.

I hung up and looked at Janet's fearful expression. I made a flippant statement like "You know Mom and her sloppy accounting. I'll get it pieced together over the weekend." This seemed to ease her as she left for the day.

How could this happen? In travel, you would payout all of the money at least 30 days prior to a trip's departure. If you purchased the tour from another tour operator, you would pay that tour operator for the tour less your negotiated commission.

Kathy came down to the travel office to see what was going on as I had the Canary Islands file in front of me verifying all passengers had paid in full. I briefed her as to my conversation and said I would have to wire them $9,200 (worth around $28,000 today) on Monday morning or else Mom and the other passengers would not be on the tour operator's return flight.

I fell silent and must have been staring blankly at Kathy because it was the worry in her voice that jerked me back to the present. "Is this the dead canary in the coal mine?"

I went on to explain that insufficient money in our main account indicated Mom had not only blown through the funds for this trip but advance deposits or full payments on future trips as well.

Depending on how extensively future trips were booked (and paid for) would determine how deeply Mom had run the business into the ground. The killer was my name was also on the business and all of the checking accounts. Regardless of whether or not I signed a single GANBC check or not, I would still be personally liable for any GANBC debts.

If ever there was a weekend from hell, this was the beginning of it. I first audited each advance reservation and verified the amount of each deposit or full payment, making sure each one of these payments made it onto a daily bank deposit sheet. What made this such a nightmare was that the money that should have been deposited into GANBC's escrow account and held until each tour's departure was instead being deposited directly into the general checking account (used to pay day-to-day operating expenses).

I cringed through the number crunching all night Friday, all day Saturday until midnight. Barring finding any cash remaining in any of the accounts which I would audit bright and early Sunday morning, from my examination of advanced deposits and payments not only had Mom used $47,000 (worth about $137,000 today) of passenger funds which should have been held in the escrow account but there were zero dollars to pay current operating expenses such as employee pays and past payroll taxes withheld from employees pay yet not transferred to the IRS or the state's division of taxation.

On Sunday morning I learned that neither Mom nor her accountant ever balanced a single month's checkbook from any of the accounts. Worse, there wasn't anything written on the check stub for a number of checks, which left no clue as to who the check was issued to or how much was paid out. I decided that if I balanced the past three years of each account it would provide me with some reasonable pattern showing where the money went and the speed with which it flowed out of the business.

Too chicken to review the general expense account where most activity occurred, I started with the lower volume accounts. I discovered they had been drained of their funds a few years ago when Len and Lynn were both running GANBC. Nothing was left. Next up, the smaller active accounts. Each one had been stripped clean. Sunday afternoon I brazenly took on the biggie: the general expense account.

Having gone back three years I could tell by the handwriting that Len had worked on maintaining a running checkbook balance in spite of missing check stub information in terms of amounts or who the checks were issued to. I saw Mom's handwriting on stubs with the payee XYZ Tours in weird amounts. One example had a tour operator being paid $1,478 for 27 GANBC members touring Santo Domingo. Now I am far short of being travel expert Arthur Frommer but I can guarantee even at 1980 rates, 27 people were not going to Santo Domingo for a week at a casino resort including air for $55 each. The actual amount on the check $14,780, a difference of $13,302 from the $1,478 entered on the stub.

Over the three year audit I only found 7 or 8 of these hefty erroneously entered transactions but they added up to drain the operating account dry and add to the present uncertain financial situation. Smaller wrong entries were along the lines of XYZ Hotel for a Pennsylvania Dutch tour: $219 instead of $2,190. The task of pulling missing stub information from the actual checks and writing it on the stub was arduous. There were smaller amounts Mom would use for personal expenses: $32 to Stop & Shop for card players, $358 to XYZ Appliances for a new refrigerator, $24 to Gerry's Liquors for card players. Checks galore issued for cash as though this was Mom's piggy bank.

My pettiness caused me to fume more over the smaller expenses, the "for the card players", than the bigger losses: the thought that I would have to bite the bullet and be forced to pick up the food and beverage tab for these career gamblers irked me.

By the end of the day on Sunday, having spent the weekend forensically trying to reconstruct the past three years of GANBC, I arrived at the figure of losses to be in the neighborhood of $161,000 plus the $47,000 of non-escrowed advanced trip money or $208,000. In today's money, GANBC was over $750,000 in the hole.

When Kathy came downstairs to check on me, I told her I didn't know whether to throw up or smash my head against the wall. After I explained the extent of GANBC's financial black hole and how I was going to be held personally liable despite never having written a GANBC check, my optimistic Kathy said she was positive I would find a way to dig us out. I remember thinking, this girl doesn't have a clue.

I turned off the lights and headed upstairs to our apartment, my mind on a continuous loop: 208 grand…208 grand…208 grand.

At bedtime I knew it would be a useless effort to try to sleep but I went to bed anyway in order not to worry Kathy. Hours into sleeplessness I shot out of bed. I had forgotten all about the money market accounts I had set up for the business a few years ago.

Searching the offices at 3AM proved unproductive. There was not even a trace of these accounts. No problem, I would call one of the account managers of GANBC's money market funds before I left for the bank to wire the Canary Islands money in the morning.

There were four money market accounts: One for $100,000 and three for $50,000 each plus any accumulated interest. However, according to the account manager I spoke to, all had been closed over the past two years. He said he would fax me the information showing where the funds from the closed accounts had been wired. After I hung up, feeling as though all of the oxygen had been vacuumed out of my body, I sat and stared at the phone, expecting him to call back any minute to say he had made a mistake and all of the accounts were active. The call never came.

By the time the doors opened at the bank that handled all GANBC and a couple of my own business accounts, I had already logged in twenty minutes of anxiety sitting in their parking lot. The manager greeted me and wanted to know the special occasion, since it would always be a staff member handling routine banking.

After I told him about my Friday telephone call from the Boston-based tour operator and what I had discovered over the weekend, I swear his voice jumped an octave when he asked what I was going to do. I gave him the information needed to wire the Canary Islands trip money to the tour operator and instructed him from which of my accounts to withdraw the funds. I then opened a new account for Great Age Corp. with only Kathy and I allowed to sign checks.

Next I closed all GANBC accounts with the exception of the general expense account, which still had outstanding checks to be processed and paid. I deposited money into this general account from my business account and told the manager to cover all GANBC checks and not return any due to insufficient funds.

When I left the bank, I wondered where the $208,000 missing from current accounts and the $250,000 in closed money market accounts went. A total of $458,000 or more than $1.5 million today. How can you blow through 1.5 million over three years?

Just the thought of going back to the office panicked me.

I drove past The Big House to have coffee alone at Dunkin' Donuts. My mind was totally frazzled. I tried to process Friday's phone call, the weekend audit, the $208,000 deficit, and the $250,000 siphoned from the money market accounts. How could my own mother suffocate GANBC? Not to mention misappropriate GANBC passengers' funds by not depositing them in an escrow account?

I thought of the people working in the office. They always appeared busy. Even Kathy's mom worked there occasionally. Years later I found out they were paid in points as opposed to money. Like Bertha and Elsa, if they worked for so many Miss Lynn points, of course subject to change without notice, they were "allowed" to escort a GANBC trip.

Angela, a long time friend and point-paid worker, told me she worked full time for an entire summer so that she could escort a trip to Las Vegas and bring Jack, her husband, as a guest. (That's the same Jack who was best man at our wedding.)

As the Vegas departure date grew closer, Angela met with Mom, who told her she had earned enough points to make her trip free, but Jack's trip would have to be paid for. Angela refused to be bullied and forced Mom to stand by her agreement that if Angela worked forty hours a week during the ten weeks of summer, Jack's trip would be complimentary along with hers. Mom backed down and did not charge for Jack.

Since that particular tour had over 50 paid passengers, the tour company operating the tour allowed 1 free with 25 so Angela, who worked the tour, and Jack's trip were freebies anyway.

As I sat at Dunkin Donuts, ten minutes into my pity party, I started to rapidly jot down notes on a napkin:

Great Age begins right now.

All telephones answered "Thank you for calling GANBC /GREAT AGE." Until GANBC debts are paid off then Mom can run GANBC again with my name removed from the corporation and especially the bank accounts.

Effective immediately all trips are to be booked on GREAT AGE invoices. Previous bookings are to be re-booked as GREAT AGE.

Starting today, all money is to be deposited into a GREAT AGE escrow account.

All checks will be signed by me. If I am away on a business trip, Kathy will be the only other person authorized to sign checks. Never Mom.

The concentration will be on tours we can operate ourselves at a higher profit margin rather than buying tours from other tour operators and working for commission.

For the foreseeable future, I have the final say in all business matters of both GREAT AGE and what remains of GANBC.

The three miles back to the office literally felt like seconds, I was so eager to get back and implement my changes, my vision. Entering the downstairs office, I asked someone to call Kathy down to cover the phones while I met with everyone in the back office. As I started the meeting, there was a look of fear in many eyes. All of them had been subjected to regular Miss Lynn conniption fits during meetings at some time or other. Now they were expecting the wrath of the warlock.

I first assured everyone that from now on we would all be working in a professional business environment. The loosey-goosey, fly by the seat of your pants GANBC days were over. My napkin notes were produced and met with excitement and approval. More than one person grimaced at Number 7 about my having the final say. Another boldly said, "Good luck with that one."

Maybe it was false hopes but everyone seemed energized even though they had probably attended more than their share of "rah, rah, we're changing things for the better here at GANBC" rallies. The only difference was this time I was the one in charge. It was a first. In the past I'd made it clear that my focus was on my own business. Now they were seeing me in a different light. My inner thought: if only they knew.

I had come to despise all aspects of travel and had been forced into this role by circumstance certainly not by desire.

I spent the rest of the day pensively: GANBC was 208 grand in the hole... being put on life support would be a step up for this dying enterprise...what type of tour products can we offer immediately to bring in money, a lot of money? It was evident that the business my mother had been running was a disaster. She was stuck in the old way of booking trips to exotic foreign locals. Reality was that fewer and fewer people were booking these types of trips.

Later that night I called Madeline, one of our older tour escorts, and asked her to stop by a few senior citizen centers the next morning to pick up any fliers promoting one day bus trips. I had Paragon, Collette and Conway Tours current overnight/multi-day bus tour catalogues brought up to me from the downstairs office.

By the end of the night I concluded it made fiscal sense to only offer our own tours. Our profits would be limited only by the prices our competition would be charging for similar tours. No more booking expensive trips and settling for a measly 10% commission. Instead we would offer competitively priced bus trips, controlled by us, and yielding 30% or more profit margins.

As soon as Madeline dropped off the senior centers' day trip brochures the next morning, I was on the phone arranging our own tours to the popular area destinations offered by senior groups. I spent the day handling the arrangements (booking buses, restaurants and attractions) to six of these locations, as well as an overnight trip to an Atlantic City non-casino hotel. Because the local tour operators had had years of business relationships with Atlantic City casinos, it was impossible to secure rooms at the rates they offered our competition. Consequently, my only option was to offer non-casino rooms.

Operating an advertising agency had its benefits, like being able to crank out typesetting and artwork almost instantaneously. In 1980, "desktop publishing" on a "computer"? Not even on the event horizon.

By the Wednesday after hell weekend and the day Miss Lynn was due to arrive back from the Canary Islands, our printer had Great Age's very first flier of bus trips on his press. I briefed our office staff on each trip and encouraged them to contact our most loyal travelers to offer them the tours before we offered them to the public. (Sell scarcity.) A number of our travelers came right into the office after receiving our telephone call to book and pay for their bus tours.

I called Mom's accountant, who lacked any initials after his name like CPA, to arrange an afternoon meeting. I confronted him over the financial records and reports he had submitted over the past three years, showing GANBC as "breaking even" when the bank statements showed it was hemorrhaging money, and how 'bout them money market funds? He claimed he worked off the figures Miss Lynn and Len gave him. When he would question Miss Lynn, she could never find the information. "It's like she couldn't find her ass with both her hands."

Laughing at his comment despite the dire situation, I agreed that it must have been extremely difficult dealing with my mother; thanked him for his past service and told him my accountants would be handling our future accounting needs.

The office staff labeled hundreds of the newly printed Great Age brochures and popped them into the mail. Based solely on their phone efforts, by the end of Great Age's first sales day, each of the six new one day bus trips had sold one-third to one-half of available seats and the one Atlantic City over-nighter was practically sold out.

Not a bad day.

I heard Mom arriving back home some time after 1AM and knew she would not be down to the office much before noon. This would enable the office staff to handle the morning burst of new bookings and allow me to contact the restaurants, attractions and our bus company to add additional buses to each trip.

The GANBC/GREAT AGE phone lines started lighting up like a Christmas tree early Thursday morning. I know this because we had Comm-Key phones with ten incoming lines installed throughout the offices and even in our apartment with the ringer shut off. It was like getting hit with a bolt of energy to see the glimmer of flashing lights from the end table in our living room. That novelty of having a business phone in the apartment wore off very quickly in the days that followed, as the twinkling lights continued late into the evening and hours before the office opened. It was a sign we were on the right track. People wanted what we were selling.

Sometime around noon, Hurricane Lynn struck first in the downstairs office before storming her way to my third floor office. She flung a handful of newly-printed Great Age brochures at me.

"What do you think you're doing? How dare you do all this while I was away! You're trying to steal my business right out from under me, junior. I'm calling my lawyer and want you and that wife of yours out of here."

I told her I understood her being upset since I myself had recently been upset by the call from her Canary Islands tour operator telling me he was staring at a bounced GANBC check.

"He's lying. There's plenty of money in that account unless you stole that too."

I continued on to explain that after a quick review of all the accounts over the weekend, the business was in the red to the tune of $208,000.

"You're not my accountant. My accountant always tells me the business is doing great."

I told her of my meeting with her "accountant" and how he was feeding reports back to her based on the information she fed to him.

"He's lying too. You're all lying. Now I know you're all in cahoots to steal my business and my money."

When I brought up the missing money from the money market accounts, she slammed her fist on my desk and told me that it was none of my goddamn business what she did with her money.

"I want you and that wife of yours out of here today."

The conversation was going nowhere. Having heard enough, I said I would happily put GANBC back together for her. All she had to do is come up with $47,000 to cover the money missing from her escrow account for trips people had under deposit or already paid in full. Plus the $9,200 I had to personally wire to get everyone back from the Canary Islands. And don't forget the payroll taxes for the past six months that hadn't been escrowed.

She could also easily rid herself of Kathy and me by returning my half of the deposit for The Big House. I was not interested in the present value of the property. All I wanted was my deposit back so I could add it to the money we were saving for a deposit on a house of our own.

As Mom stormed out of my office, she said I would be hearing from David, her lawyer.

I called after her, "David, your heart surgeon?"

David, the imaginary love of her life, was alive and well. He must have tired of being a surgeon and gone for his law degree.

An hour or so later I received a call from a man purportedly representing my mother, ordering me to return all of the funds that I had stolen from her accounts or he would seek an immediate court order to have me removed from the premises. After giving him my business attorney's name, I encouraged him to proceed with a lawsuit. This gave him pause, and he asked me how I could be so glib and why I would want to go this route. I informed the good counselor that I had 208 thousand reasons. He said this left him no option but to see me in court.

I agreed that this would probably be the best route for all of us, but just before I hung up I commented, "I suggest you get your retainer fee from Miss Lynn upfront."

Was he a legitimate legal eagle? Who knows? No court case was ever filed. At least not over the past 30 years.

It didn't take long before the icy relationship between Mom and me began to thaw. I can't say it was anything I did. It was more like she was suddenly becoming aware of the tremendous volume (and cash) now flowing through the formerly dying office.

There were two to four buses heading to Atlantic City each week, or twelve buses rolling up to a Massachusetts coastal town for a clambake, or nine buses leaving for New Hampshire or Vermont every Saturday and Sunday during the foliage season.

We reached a consensus: All air tours would end after we honored the tours already on our books (the $47,000 of advance reservations). I made a few concessions that wouldn't impact the overall business. For example, I did not have a problem giving in to Miss Lynn's request that our tour escorts continued to wear an orange poncho-type top over tan slacks.

Since advertising our tours through mass media outlets (television, radio and local newspapers) was prohibited at the time by state law (due to the fact we were technically only allowed to offer our tours to our members), I had an idea to expand our one or two page newsletter listing trips to our 5,000 member base: our own newspaper called *Great News*. To hammer down the cost of a mailed newspaper, we sought Second Class or Periodical Status with the U.S. Post Office.

The problem with this is we could not put out a periodical type publication containing nothing but our tour programs as it would have to have other content to qualify as a periodical. Mom would write a column of special interest to seniors and we would fill the rest of the content area of the paper with varying topics and special columns. The greatest benefits of using a monthly newspaper format were the flexibility to keep adding new tour offerings and the ability to cost-effectively reach our members regularly.

Outside advertisers eager to reach the senior citizen market started calling us to advertise in *Great News*. I assigned Mom to call on these advertisers and sell them ad space while she was out promoting free Great Age memberships at senior meetings. Not only did it give her a sense of accomplishment, but it gave the downstairs office staff a break from Miss Lynn going all Miss Lynn on them and those members out front booking tours.

My style of operating the Great Age travel business (by repeating the same trip over and over again without variation) proved to be financially successful. At that point, I projected it would take me only a couple of years to bring the business to where it should have been financially before the Canary Islands telephone call, my wake-up call that the canary was about to die in the mineshaft.

Once this was accomplished I would be able to return to the *sane* insane world of advertising and marketing. And return GANBC back to Mom with a clean balance sheet. She would then be able to resurrect her air tour business without the annoying bus trips which she loathed and, more importantly, without me.

The *only* potential roadblock to my plan: Miss Lynn.

11. On the Road Again

"What the hell did you do?" Maureen said as she walked into my office. She could not believe how crazy busy the downstairs office was. I told her all I was doing was making widgets: Creating tours was like manufacturing the same widgets time after time after time, with no defects and no deviations.

It had been a couple of years since Maureen and her family moved to Florida. When she left, it was like losing a big sister, but we did keep in touch. I had known she would be up to visit her family in Rhode Island this summer; however I wasn't expecting her today.

Over lunch she told me she and her husband had divorced and she was thinking of moving back to Rhode Island with one of her daughters to be closer to her family. I told her if she moved back I would offer her a position to head tour operations, which involved packaging our tours, securing and training tour escorts and overseeing the smooth operation of all tours.

Having experienced Miss Lynn's erratic personality over the years, Maureen was doubtful at first until I assured her that I was in complete control of Great Age. I had brought marketing and financial stability to the business and would continue to do so.

Continue? Had I just made a commitment to stay with Great Age? What about "Two years and I'm out of here?" I decided not to worry about it. Maybe Maureen won't leave Florida and I won't feel compelled to stay beyond my self-imposed two-year stint.

It's possible I was a tad overly enthusiastic at lunch, because in a matter of a month Maureen was my second-in-command.

From that point on, Mom and I used Maureen as a buffer between, well, Mom and me. It was Maureen who endured the screaming Miss Lynn in the basement and the raging Andy over the latest, greatest Miss Lynn caper on the third floor. Surprisingly, she didn't quit.

Saturday morning of Labor Day weekend in 1981, Mom and a busload of our passengers were getting ready to board the parked bus in front of The Big House for a three-day trip to Hickey's in Vermont. At the same time I was helping a very pregnant Kathy carefully down the stairs and into the car. We were on our way to Women and Infants Hospital for the birth of our first child.

When the tour bus arrived at their Vermont hotel, the passengers on Mom's bus started to applaud. Hotel owners Donna and Jim Hickey had posted "Miss Lynn, It's a girl!" on their hotel's large exterior sign.

We had started to limit the occasions Mom could go out on tour because of her bizarre behavior. In Reality According to Miss Lynn, she ruled supreme, barking out orders to hotel management, restaurant staff and destination tour guides or attractions, treating them as her personal servants. More often than not her grandiose attitude would intimidate and quell any hint of dissent. Miss Lynn swept all before her.

Mom met her match and received her comeuppance escorting a Pennsylvania Dutch Country tour. Her name was Lydia, and she was a lovely, older local tour guide assigned to Miss Lynn's passengers.

MISS LYNN: Do you know who I am?

LYDIA *(sweetly)*: No, dear, but I'm sure we'll find out and let you know by the end of the tour.

MISS LYNN: I don't like your attitude. I'm Miss Lynn. I started this business years ago. And I have the power to never have you on any of my buses ever.

LYDIA: Pleased to meet you, darlin'. I've been a local Pennsylvania Dutch Country tour guide for over 40 years. I have the power to never board one of your buses ever again. Enough power to make sure no other Penn Dutch guide will board any of your buses ever. Hon, why don't you take a seat so we can start the tour for these wonderful folks?

When the tour returned home, some passengers on Mom's bus phoned our office to complain about Miss Lynn's rude treatment of that sweet Penn Dutch tour guide; a few stated they would not travel with us in the future if Miss Lynn was their tour escort.

Later, when it came time to raise the subject with my mother, I anticipated the usual vituperative denial and shifting of blame to anyone but herself. She did not disappoint. She then demanded to know which passengers had called in, because she wanted to call them and set them straight. Great, let's lose even more business. As soon as I refused to give her the information, she turned it into a personal attack against me: "...no one called; you're lying to make me look bad. I'll show you, I'm going to call every single passenger to prove you're lying."

Clearly any rational business person would restrict this unstable individual from having any customer contact whatsoever. But she was my mother, and we quickly learned to stack the deck by assigning her to buses we would make every effort to fill with travelers who liked traveling with her.

There were certain peak periods where all components to a typical tour – transportation, accommodations and attractions – are in the highest demand and all tour guides are on duty: Memorial Day Weekend, Labor Day Weekend and New Year's Eve. One of the bus companies we chartered a coach from for a New Year's Eve tour requested to know ahead of time who would be the escort on their bus. Remembering previous problems Miss Lynn had had with one of their drivers, we said escort assignments were still up in the air, even though we had already assigned Mom to one of their buses and had filled it with people who knew her. The bus company rep proceeded to make things perfectly clear. "It had better not be Miss Lynn. We will pull the bus once it arrives at the [designated passenger] pick-up area if she is the escort.

We were one of the first to purchase an IBM dumb (without any internal data storage) desktop computer when they were introduced by the former ComputerLand outlets around 1980. Along with this we also bought a Corvus external hard disk drive to store both our tour reservations and growing mailing list of over 17,000 Great Age members.

While Great Age was making quite a name for itself with its explosive growth, Miss Lynn was making a name for herself with her explosive temper, both in the office and while escorting passengers on tour.

The following spring, Kathy was pregnant with our second child, and we were fast outgrowing our second floor apartment. It was time to start looking for a place of our own, big enough to house our growing family.

When I told Mom about our decision, she offered us the first floor and the second floor, which could be easily converted into four bedrooms. Mom would move into the studio apartment on the first floor. We were against it. We thought Mom would feel too confined in such a small space, but she insisted she would be fine since she spent most of her time in her office when she wasn't on the road. (The office also had a backroom – sans shower curtain - which had been permanently set-up as "Miss Lynn's Poker Parlor" for her once or twice weekly poker games.)

At that time neither Mom nor I were deriving any income from the travel business. She made around $2,000 a month from hosting her poker games (comparable to around $5,600 per month today); and my income still came from my advertising and marketing firm. I had set up this arrangement so we could pay our bills when due, pay our employees on time, and chip away at the massive GANBC debt, which would be paid off completely by mid-summer, 1982.

Mom insisted on doing back-to-back (one trip right after the other) tours to "Hickey's in Vermont," because she could put on the fun Miss Lynn "just look at the business I built" persona with both the passengers and the Hickeys, as well. Although Donna Hickey would frequently call me about Miss Lynn, she also thought she was fun and would keep her bus passengers entertained.

It worked out to be a financial windfall for both Mom and her tour bus driver, as their tips, in addition to their pay, would exceed the average of $5 per passenger per three day trip or around $240 per bus times twice each week starting in the spring right through the fall. Mom would realize another $2,000+ per month in tips. Her monthly income during this time: $2,000 (cash) per month from Miss Lynn's Poker Palace, $2,000 (cash) per month from tour tips and $1,800 per month in tour escort pay…worth $16,000 per month in today's dollars. She would claim in future letters that she was penniless during this time period, which I suppose was true when compared to the "$1.5 million" she'd managed to squander in three short years before I was forced to take control of the business' finances.

She would later tell friends and relatives how she was taken off the company's payroll which is also true, both of us were. However she failed to mention Great Age was providing her with over $3,850 each month (when you remove her poker revenue). She also didn't mention that I wasn't being paid anything.

During the warm months, I would ask Mom to please use the outside stairs from her apartment to the pool on the days she was home in between the Hickey's tours. Of course she refused, mortifying the office crew by prancing through the office – dripping wet and oiled up - to use the inside stairway instead. They felt it was highly unprofessional and made us look like a schlock organization. I couldn't have agreed with them more. However, I knew from many years of dealing with Mom that no one was going to tell her what to do. Period.

Mom was an animal lover, probably where I get it from, and always had a dog or cat in our household. Since it was impractical to have a dog with its daily feeding and outdoor needs given her on-the-road schedule, Mom had a cat. No, not a cat, three cats: Bobby, Pretty and Frisky. While Bobby and Pretty did their thing once they were let out in the morning, Frisky would prefer to come into the office as soon as it opened like it was his job. Most times he would lie on the window sill and stare indifferently at those mere mortals booking their tours. Other times Frisky would get, well, frisky.

Because our *Great News* newspaper was classified by the U.S. Post Office as a Second Class publication, we had an annual audit in our office in which a postal inspector could examine any record related to our subscriber/member base. Another component of this audit would be a random selection of two to four *Great News* monthly editions over the previous year in order to verify compliance with their news content to advertising ratio.

Whenever the postal agent visited, I would be notified and, if Miss Lynn was not out on a tour, I would ask her to stay out of this meeting, fearing her biting responses to matter-of-fact questioning by our visiting postal authority. Financially, too much was on the line for an abrasive Miss Lynn to blow our Second Class mailing status.

Mom would usually comply. However, during one inspection I am convinced Mom sent her operative, Frisky, to take her place. Over one of the file cabinets in the front office, a ceiling tile was left slightly askew to provide the featherweight Frisky with a means to access his passageway to the world or at least the other basement offices.

Colleen, the postal inspector was sitting at a back office desk far away from the flurry of activity in the front. I was sitting across the desk from Colleen, my stomach churning, worried that a dripping Mom would stop by to chat.

A creaking ceiling tile overhead caught my attention. I looked up expecting to see a tile bending under Frisky's weight. Although there was no weight related depression in any of the foam tiles, I did notice one tile directly over where Colleen was working move slightly from its frame. Damn Frisky. Damn his claws. Helpless, I watched as he worked the tile open. Go way. Get away. I'll give you a treat after Colleen leaves, Frisky. Go. Go.

THUD.

Frisky landed neatly on Colleen's ledger book and started to nuzzle her under her chin. Apologizing profusely, I made a grab for Frisky, but Colleen waved me away and began petting him. She apparently had two cats of her own. For the rest of the audit Frisky laid sprawled on the desk next to Colleen, occasionally stretching out a paw to seize Colleen's pen, glaring at me as if to say, Try grabbing me again, buster, and Colleen will flunk your sorry ass.

Every night since our daughter Kristen's birth, Kathy and I were at home with our newborn. In August, just before her first birthday I convinced Kathy that we should get out for a night to see a live show at the Warwick Musical Theater. Eleanor, our day time babysitter during the school year, encouraged us to go and have a good time. She would be happy to come over and stay with Kristen.

Mom arrived home late in the afternoon from one of her tours and visited with Kathy and Kristen. When Kathy told her we were going to the theater, Mom insisted Kathy call Eleanor to tell her she would be babysitting instead. Against Kathy's better judgment, and mine as soon as I heard about the change in plans, we decided to leave Kristen with her grandmother since it would only be for a few hours.

At intermission, we were the first at the pay telephones. We called our house phone. No answer. We called Mom's phone. No answer. We called the business lines. No answer.

With flashers on, I drove like a maniac while we discussed all possible scenarios, positive and negative. As soon as we arrived home we caught sight of Mom walking toward us from the pool area with Kristen wrapped in a towel. I took the baby from Mom and handed her to Kathy while Mom asked, "What's the problem with you two?"

I looked at her without saying a word. I had not calmed down yet from our sheer terror of something having happened to our daughter.

"The baby wanted to dangle her legs in the pool, what's wrong with that?"

Even though the pool had two side lights, our daughter could have slipped underwater at a number of unlit areas and drowned while we were 12 miles away on our first night out since she arrived on this earth.

What actually transpired that night and what Mom told others about how badly her son treated her in front of his wife were two diametrically different stories. Her version had her rocking our daughter gently to sleep, and upon hearing the phone, deciding to let it ring through so our sleepy daughter would not get startled and wake up.

Our friend, Lucille, who had been renting the second floor studio apartment, married her soul mate that summer. Since both businesses were more than covering the property's expenses, and now that my family's bedrooms were across the hall and the computer, along with sensitive business data was just above, we needed more privacy. Mom and I agreed to leave the apartment empty.

Many times Mom would return from a tour with bunches of paper and instruct one of our reservationists to process the scribbled bookings into our system. When these *firm* reservations were contacted to make a deposit, we would learn that Miss Lynn discussed the trips with them but they had never agreed to book them. Worse were the times she would come in after a senior center meeting and reserve full buses for various destinations. This would trigger tour operations into chartering buses, blocking the rooms at destination hotels, and lining up restaurants and attractions, only to learn the group leader never really intended to book these tours. Tour operations would then have to cancel the arrangements thereby damaging our reputation.

I finally sent a memo. No reservations taken by Miss Lynn, either for individual trips or full buses, were to be entered into our reservation system until they were under deposit, as everyone else had to do. As soon as Mom saw my memo, she was in my office, once again explaining that the business was hers, and she would do what she damn well pleased. And I once again reminded her that the unofficially bankrupt GANBC was her business, and I had to maintain tight financial control, including complete control over what qualifies as a reservation – a deposit upfront - and what qualifies for a person's wish list reservation.

Mom then insisted I write a new memo saying that all of Miss Lynn's reservations were to be entered into our system. I told her I would absolutely do that for her: All of Miss Lynn's hypothetical reservations would be inputted into a hypothetical computer for hypothetical trips that were never going to happen.

This yuletide confrontation took place in mid December. A few days before Christmas Mom left a Christmas gift for Kristen outside our front door. In spite of Kathy trying to get me to make peace with Mom, especially given the season, I refused. We had been locking horns ever since the Canary Islands debacle: While I was trying to keep the business and our financial lives afloat, she kept throwing obstacles in my way, bucking my every move.

I left her Christmas gifts from us on the desk in her downstairs office.

When Christmas Day arrived, I was the first to blink and knocked on her door to invite her over to see her granddaughter open up her gifts from Santa. Although she was home, she did not respond.

While our wide-eyed toddler gleefully unwrapped packages, we could hear Mom making loud telephone calls from her house phone recounting how vile her son and daughter-in-law were by not letting her see her own grandchild on Christmas morning. Although this upset Kathy, I had lived with these bogus calls to imaginary friends or relatives all my life. I turned up the volume of the Christmas carols playing on our stereo.

It was my dad's family tradition to have a get together around noon on New Year's Day to celebrate the New Year by personally wishing each other health and success. Once Kathy and I married, we began hosting this New Year's Day brunch. In spite of it being all of Dad's side, we would always extend an invitation to Mom to join us if she was not out on a tour. She would always decline, "You people enjoy the day with Big Andrew and *the other end*."

The New Year's Day following her Christmas Day proclamation about her despicable son and that wife of his, we once again invited her to join us, and she once again declined. Once *the other end* was gathered together, the jovial holiday atmosphere was pierced by the sound of Miss Lynn's voice in loud conversation with David, the imaginary love of her life. It appeared that David was planning to stop by. She was thrilled and happy to hear it. Her real message, of course, was to let *the other end* know that she had indeed climbed to the pinnacle of the social strata: A beau who was a business executive AND a lawyer AND a heart surgeon. Eat your heart out, Big Andrew.

Anticipating her maneuver, I had carried the stereo from the living room into the foyer prior to our guests arriving. I turned the volume up a tad and we got on with our festivity. A while later, I saw her drive off, perhaps to meet David, perhaps to meet up with other fictitious friends.

A week later, we dropped Kristen off at Dad and Val's and continued on to the hospital for our son's birth a few minutes before midnight. After leaving the hospital I stopped at Dunkin Donuts to savor the moment over a cup of coffee before proceeding to the pay phone and making two calls about the birth of our Matthew: One to Dad and the other to Mom.

Here's how my conversation with Mom went:
MOM: Hello.
ME: Hi, Mom. It's me.
MOM: Who?
ME: Your son.
MOM: What is it?
ME: Kathy just had the baby. It's a boy.
MOM (*hangs up*)

At that point in my life, I was used to Mom hanging up on me. Maybe I read too much into it, but as I was driving to Dad's, I thought, Honey, you just hung up on my newborn son, our family, and your future involvement in our lives.

Once we were all back home, Mom did stop by to "get a look" at Matthew. The ice cold visit rivaled the piled January snow outside.

The Big House came with an antiquated steam heating system complete with clanging radiators and whooshes of escaping steam. There were many nights when the ancient, enormous boiler would literally run out of steam and I would have to manually refill it with water. We would realize this when the inside temperature would rapidly start to drop. Thus started many nights of getting up in our second floor bedroom and making my way down the back stairs to the first floor. There I would have to unlock Mom's door and walk across her hallway to the stairs leading down to the basement.

The night after we returned home with our daughter and newborn son, the boiler consumed all of the water in its system by 3AM. I got up, grabbed the key to Mom's apartment and headed downstairs. I had a difficult time getting the key into the lock, and when I finally forced it, it wouldn't budge. What the hell? I went back upstairs, bundled up, and went outside to gain access through the office entrance. Once the boiler's thirst was satisfied, I fired it up, retraced my steps and went back to bed.

When I told Mom about the problem with the lock, she told me there was no problem. The lock had been changed and I was no longer allowed to use the inside stairway off her hallway to the basement. No other conversation I ever had with my mother is etched more vividly in my mind than the one we had over the locked door:

ME: You mean to tell me that you would let your granddaughter and infant grandson freeze?
MOM: Don't look at me, junior. Look in the mirror; you and your wife caused the problem not me.
ME: So you would let them freeze?
MOM: That's not the point. The point is how bad you people treat me.
ME: You could never call yourself a mother. Now you'll never be able to call yourself a grandmother.

If it were only Kathy and me, I would have simply cranked up our heating blanket and tended to the boiler in the morning. But I didn't want our two cherubs to be chilled, so I continued to brave the cold and icy winter nights to keep my family warm. Don't think

I didn't land on my butt more than once on the icy stairs or the walkway leading around the house to the basement door, either.

When you're Catholic what normally occurs a month or so after the birth of a child is the baby's baptism. Matthew's took place on the first Sunday in February. Although we invited Mom to the church ceremony, she did not attend. She sort of didn't attend the celebration party we held back at the house, either. I say "sort of" because she was back in position on the other side of the locked door in the foyer. Another loud phone call, this time about not being included in "my own grandson's baptism." The stereo's volume was once again ratcheted up.

What followed next was a volley of written messages pitched under the foyer door, some of them reaching clear across the floor to where some of our guests were standing and chatting. It must have made her crazy when no one paid the least attention. The only time the notes were picked up was after the party when we swept them up to put in the trash. I glanced at one sitting on top of the pile: "I am the only, true blood-grandmother"

In the winter, our Atlantic City tours kept the business alive. We were sending four or five busloads each week, and I had Maureen schedule our best escorts to keep them working during a Northeast tour operator's worse time of year. Mom had another idea. She thought these trips should be assigned to her and not *strangers*.

During one of these confrontations in early February, Mom was up in our office demanding that our escorting schedule be revamped to include her on one of the weekly Atlantic City trips. She was getting bored being off the road.

I offered a compromise. Knowing how much she loved to gamble, I suggested that she travel as one of our passengers to Atlantic City at no cost to her. She refused unless she received the escort's tip money. This blew me away. You want to take the tip money due the tour escort who is working the trip? Rather than once again fighting irrationality, I turned to Maureen and instructed her to leave the schedule exactly as it was and walked away.

Miss Lynn stayed in front of Maureen's desk and tried to bully this friend of many years into bumping one of our better tour conductors for her. Maureen refused. Miss Lynn then asked Maureen why she was not doing what she'd been ordered to do.

Maureen answered with another quiet "no." When pressed further, I overheard Maureen say, "Lynn, to be honest with you, Andy thinks you're inconsistent when you escort." After absorbing the initial shock of discovering Maureen had a voice, Miss Lynn asked Maureen if she agreed with my assessment and Maureen said, "Yes."

If ever a shot was fired and heard around the world that "Yes" was it. Before she left, Mom blustered that she was now going to team up with her fabulously wealthy Wall Streeter friend, David, and crush our Mickey Mouse operation. "Both of you will be begging me to take you back, don't waste your breath."

I went over to a quivering Maureen and said, "I didn't realize you were such a diplomat." Then I told her my mother was partially correct in saying we were a Mickey Mouse operation. Not in the sense she used the term, but in the sense of operating our growing business out of the basement of a house, albeit The Big House. We would have to locate retail office space as soon as possible, preferably in the nearby city of Cranston.

That afternoon and in the days following, I drove along many busy Cranston streets looking for a retail level location without any success. There were plenty of second floor locations but no ground level storefronts were available.

Valentine's Day was the following week and Eleanor insisted that Kathy and I go out while she took care of Kristen and Matthew. After we dined, the romantic evening continued with a ride up and down one of the state's busiest streets, Reservoir Avenue in Cranston, searching for a storefront location to rent. Never let it be said that I don't know how to woo a woman.

Just as we decided to head home, Kathy spotted a "For Lease" sign in the window of a three unit retail building. That window had been covered with brown paper when I'd driven by it the day before. I had assumed it was a remodeling project.

We got out of the car and looked through the large windows and realized this would be a perfect location for our tour business. I wrote down the telephone number on the "For Lease" sign.

The next morning I called the number around 7AM, expecting to get an answering machine requesting me to leave my name and number. Instead, a wide-awake sounding gentleman with a Greek accent answered the phone, and I told him that I'd like to make an appointment to see the retail space on Reservoir Avenue.

Half an hour later we were standing in the space of our future tour operator retail office at 508 Reservoir Avenue. I gave our new landlord Teddy a security deposit and the first month's rent, and he gave me a set of keys. I mentioned that I hoped to open our doors on March 2nd, which was less than two weeks away. He thought that to be rather ambitious, considering the space was a shell, but then again he didn't know about the hellish conditions we were conducting our business from presently.

I caught Maureen before she left home for the office and asked her to stop by 508 Reservoir Avenue, Cranston, and I'd pick up some coffee for us.

As she entered the building, her first words were, "This is our new office, isn't it?"

Once inside I gave a quick layout overview: desk, desk, desk, counter, computer area, back office desk, desk, storage, rest room. As we stood there, sharing a mutual blissful feeling of finally being able to operate Great Age in peace, I dropped the next bit of news.

Since Great Age catered solely to the senior market, I had been tossing around a way to market our tours to all age groups. It would involve a name change. We would be known as "Hartley Tours," with the slogan, "We put our heart in all our tours."

Not sure what Maureen thought of this at first. Was she quietly staring at a marketing genius or a village idiot? Her response, "What the hell took you so long to come up with that?

Although we would not be abandoning Great Age completely - it would continue as our vehicle to market to seniors along with its *Great News* newspaper - the outside signage and inside décor of the office would reflect the Hartley Tours moniker.

We returned to the Union Avenue office, and Maureen told staffers as they arrived about our shooting for a March 2nd office relocation. I went upstairs to tell Kathy the end result of our previous night's amorous Reservoir Avenue drive before I ventured downstairs to tell Mom what was going on.

After telling her about leasing the new location, I assured her that even though space would be tight, she would, of course, have her own desk there. She said that wouldn't be necessary. She had already been working on resurrecting GANBC, not as GANBC, but as "Lynn Simmons Tours". Her focus would be on selling the air tour packages, which had made her so successful in the past. Successful, right. If I hadn't stepped in, along with losing The Big House, GANBC would be as dead as our financial reputations. Mom continued that she was happy to have us out of there, leaving the downstairs office space for herself and "my people"

With an eye toward franchising, my focus on this first Hartley Tours unit was twofold: Make it look like it was part of a huge chain of tour offices and document everything we did so we could easily replicate it when expanding with Hartley franchises and company-owned branch locations.

Monday, March 2nd finally arrived...

12. The Move

...and we were ready to officially answer our newly installed phones: "Thank you for calling Hartley Tours." The relocation had involved a coordinated night and day effort with the construction renovations done by Kathy's dad (a master carpenter) and her brother, Bob.

Our euphoria was short lived. Mom was one of the first callers and she was demanding that I return to the Union Avenue offices immediately and remove the two file cabinets tucked away in the back storage room, or she would throw the contents out. I apologized for the cabinets being such a bother to her and said I would move them upstairs into my home when I returned later that night.

Kathy cooked a meal for Maureen and me that Monday night to celebrate the office's opening. Mom was invited but said she was way too busy with Lynn Simmons Tours to join us. While we were enjoying our meal, I heard footsteps going up the back staircase. I made a beeline up our stairway and opened our second floor door leading to the outer hall and was met by a woman with two men carrying suitcases. She introduced herself and said she had rented the studio apartment that afternoon after seeing the ad in the paper. Ad in the paper? I asked her who she rented the apartment from since I owned the place. She corrected me and said that Miss Lynn is the owner and she was the one who rented it to her.

I don't recall touching a single stair en route to the downstairs office, where I was sure I would find Mom. I questioned her about what was going on and was told she had to now look out for herself. I asked what she knew of this person and did this person come with references. She told me she was a wonderful person, unlike her son and daughter-in-law.

Without responding to the personal insult, I left the office and returned to dinner, filling in Kathy and Maureen about our "wonderful person" neighbor. Over the next few days Kathy heard movement in the hall during the day. We would both hear it in the evening and concluded it was probably more of the woman's belongings being moved in.

Friday night after the office closed, the staff was organizing the day's activities when I received a frantic call from Kathy, who said there was a man banging on the door leading in from the outside to the back stairway, demanding, "Let me into the fucking place or I'll break the goddamn door down." Shaken, Kathy said he was also pounding on our front door. I told her I'd be right there. Before I left the office, I told Maureen to call the Providence Police and tell them some guy was threatening my family at our house.

My only thoughts were: What have I done to my wife? Brought her from a sane, serene and loving family into this hell hole of dysfunction, leading to her being frightened at this very moment by some aggressive weirdo. And even though she's probably petrified, I know she's got our children close by her side. I'm so sorry, Kathy.

By the time I arrived home, the guy was no longer in front of the house. I rushed in to see my traumatized wife sitting on the lower stairs, clutching our daughter and infant son. Within seconds, two squad cars were in our driveway and I went outside to provide the police with the little information I had. They asked me to unlock the door leading to the back stairs and we all went up to the "wonderful person's" apartment. Using my pass key, we walked in to find no one home. One of the officers went down the hall, turned and looked up the stairway to the third floor. Hiding on the stairs was "wonderful person" and the door-pounding guy.

Turns out the woman had a lengthy rap sheet as a prostitute, servicing the drug dealer trade in order to support her own drug addiction. Another officer turned to me and asked, "Pal, don't you research anyone you let in your house?" I briefly explained the situation. He told me that for my family's sake, I should get them out of there immediately as her other "druggie Johns" would be coming by to be serviced until word hit the streets of her arrest.

One squad car took the handcuffed "wonderful person" and her friend to the police station. The other one waited for Kathy and me to pack a few necessities for the kids. It then followed us to the interstate as we sought safety for our family at my father and Val's house.

I telephoned Maureen once we arrived at Dad's to explain what had transpired and she said for me not to worry about the office, she would cover for me on Saturday.

The following day Dad accompanied me back to The Big House to pack up additional clothing and other children necessities.

The weather was nasty; an icy rainstorm on top of snow drifts covering the storm drains, flooding the streets. Finally arriving at our Union Avenue house, we were greeted by padlocked chains shutting tight the upper and lower entrance gates to the large circular drive.

I asked Dad if he had a chain cutter. He said he had one back at his house.

We drove back, got his cutter and returned to The Big House, where I snipped the chain. After collecting the items we needed, we were exiting through the foyer when Mom sweetly called out from the other side of the locked foyer door, "Is everything all right?" I didn't say a word. Neither did Big Andrew. He did flip her off in absentia, though, which I thought was hysterical given the circumstances.

Meadow Road where Dad and Val lived was our safe house for the next week.

When we returned to Union Avenue, Dad and Val came along with us to care for the children in the event Mom had conjured up other surprises.

The locksmith arrived shortly after we did and changed the locks on our front door as well as the door to the side stairway leading up to the second floor studio apartment. Over Mom's objection I refused to let anyone, including her, have a duplicate key for the outside side stairway door.

Seeing Mom outside the following day, I confronted her about putting my family in jeopardy by renting the apartment to a drug-addicted whore. Her response was that it was her tenant, a decent woman, who was put in jeopardy. And she went on to say that she spoke to a friend of hers on the Providence Police force who told her there was nothing wrong with the woman and that we were all lying. I wanted to ask if the cop she spoke to was named David but I let it pass.

All was calm the following couple of weeks, which allowed me to head to Pennsylvania to scout out a couple of resort hotels to host our tours. My intention was to leave early and spend the first day visiting the first hotel and meeting with their sales manager to negotiate a deal. The next morning I planned to continue on to the second resort, arriving late afternoon for a dinner meeting with their sales staff before heading home the following morning.

When I received no answer at home before I left for dinner on the second night, I called the office and Maureen said everything was fine but to get in touch with Kathy as she had good news. Good news? What's that? Trying to extract any news out of Maureen was futile. She's excellent at keeping secrets. Getting back to my room after the dinner meeting, I called home and Kathy was ebullient. Hearing her so excited after the hell we had recently been through made it even more exciting for me.

That afternoon she and a few of her teacher friends had visited a house which one of the other teachers knew was for sale and thought it would be a perfect starter house for us, given our desperation to move. Though they were unable to gain access, they looked through all the windows on the first floor and agreed it would be ideal. I said I would be home late the next day and we could do a drive by when I got there. Hanging up the phone, I decided to not wait until the morning but to head home straight away.

The next morning we drove by the house and contacted the realtor, who met us there when Kathy got out of school that afternoon. Being a bank owned home, there was no negotiating on the asking price. You either paid what they wanted or moved on to another property.

Kathy and I looked at the dated shag carpeting in the living and dining rooms. We looked at the small family room which was nothing more than an enclosed breezeway with drafty sliders on either end. We looked at the hole in the door leading to the basement. We could not look at the closet door in the downstairs bedroom, as it was missing. Perhaps a solution would be a plastic shower curtain ala Miss Lynn's Beauty Salon. We looked at the three colors of paint on the outside of the house. We looked at all of it and said, "We love it. We'll take it. How quickly can we move in?"

We agreed to the bank's selling price and gave the realtor a deposit check on the spot which was accepted by the bank. The closing was scheduled for the third week in April and our move-in date was set for May 1st.

When I told my mother we were moving, she responded that we had better make sure we left the house exactly as we found it. I thought that would require spreading a truckload of filth and dirt in the place, but I nodded in agreement. Then came the zinger: Kathy should spend time cleaning the house in order for Mom to begin showing it to prospective tenants.

Kathy SPEND TIME cleaning it? Ironic, since Mom would always marvel at how immaculate our place was kept in spite of Kathy working full time and caring for a toddler and an infant.

I suggested we consider selling The Big House. The upkeep was outrageously expensive. January's gas bill for the heat alone was $797 (around $1,800 today). Mom claimed it was our fault that the bill was so high. It had never been more than $400 when she controlled the single thermostat located in the foyer on the first floor.

On moving day the movers loaded the two floors worth of furniture and boxes on the van and then loaded the remainder of our belongings which we had stored in the carriage house. Before continuing to our three-toned house in Warwick, we stopped by to say good-bye to Mom and leave her all of our keys. Based on her history of mothering, I didn't expect to hear, "Good luck in your new house." True to form, she threatened me instead: "You have to get the rest of your stuff out of your third floor office as my contractor will be converting it into my loft home right away. If your things are not out by next week, they'll be brought to the dump." Thanks, Mom, I can always count on you.

Nine months after our move, Mom demanded I turn over my GANBC Realty stock certificate representing 50% ownership in The Big House to her immediately. I told her I had no problem turning the stock certificate back to the corporation, in essence giving her full ownership of the property, and I would not even seek my original deposit back. However, I would only do this at the time of closing when someone purchases the house. Her response arrived in the mail a few days later:

February 21, 1984
"IF YOU DO NOT TURN OVER THE STOCK CERTIFICATE, (MY CERTIFICATE) FOR THE HOUSE, WITHIN TEN DAYS, TO MY LAWYER, I WILL CUT OFF EVERYTHING I OWN TO THE CHILDREN YOU ARE USING AS TOOLS, (YOUR

CHILDREN) AND A COPY OF THE WILL WILL READ AS FOLLOWS.

I LYNN M. SIMMONS WISH TO LEAVE ALL MONIES AND PROPERTY TO MY TWO BLOOD NEPHEWS, JOHN NIMMO AND THOMAS NIMMO, EQUAL SHARES. JOHN NIMMO IS THE EXECUTIVE [sic] OF MY ESTATE. $1.00 SHALL BE GIVEN TO THE MAN ANDREW J. ACCIAIOLI WHO ONCE WAS MY SON. NO OTHER CHANGES WILL BE MADE UPON MY DEATH.

THE SECON [sic] CHOICE IF MY CERTIFICATE IS TURNED OVERF TO ME SHALL READ. AS ABOVE WITH THE EXCEPTION, ALL MONIES AND ESTATE SHALLBE PUT IN TRUST FOR MY TWO GRAND CHILDREN.

SO YOUHAVE THE CHOICE, SINCE YOU STOLE THE BUSINESS FROM ME, WITH NO MONEY AND TRIED TO HAVE ME ARRESTED, I WILL TELL YOU HERE ON PAPER, I DO NOT WANT TO SEE YOU ANYMORE OR EVER HEAR FROM YOU AGAIN. YOUSHALL HEAR FROM MY ATTORNEY HEREON AND ONCE THE PROPERTY IS SETTLED AND IF IT ISNOT, I SHALL GO INTO COURT TO SUE YOU FOR STEALING MY BUSINESS. I NOW HAVE THE MONEY AND STRENGTH SO WATCH OUT. MAUREEN SURE HAS SOMETHING ON YOU AND WHEN I FIND OUT AS I SAID SOMEONE IS NEAR YOU WHO IS DOING A GREAT JOB OF INFORMING, I WILL TAKE IT FROM THERE.

GOODBYE FOREVER
LYNN SIMMONS"

...

The very next day, after joining Kathy, the children and me for dinner at our house, Mom returned to hers and authored this:

February 22, 1984 (9PM)
Dear Rusty

This is the last letter you will receive from me and the last time you will hear from me. I came to your house today because I had to see the babies also for the last time or until they are old enough, (if I live long enough) to visit me.

I was very happy to see Matthew. HE is absolutely beautiful and if you look back at some of your pictures when you were his age, you will see yourself. As for Kristen, she is gorgeous. They are both the most beautiful children in this world. I hope and pray that they will always be happy and I pray even more that they will never hurt you as you did to me. I do not believe that anyone in this world could suffer as badly as I have from the terrible things you and Kathy have done to me but GOD IS EVERYWHERE and when your children grow up, if GOD FORBID, they hurt you, you will remember what you did to your own mother. I did not intend to write about this but I must tell you why I will not be seeing you anymore and why I drove up to your house to see the children perhaps for the last time.

I have had a very bad time from the abuse you and Kathy have forced on me. I have been very ill and am fighting a battle to get well and stay well period. My doctor found it necessary for me to speak to someone who could help me from the mental anguish I have been suffering and finally I have had the help I should have had back in February and March, one year ago today.

Since my love for my son, his wife and babies have been rejected, have been cast aside as dirt, I must shift this very love to those who will not turn away from me, who will not treat me as a "rag", and who will return some love to me for without anyone's love, what is life?

Many evenings I thought how sad for mothers who lost their sons during the war. How badly they must have suffered and still suffer. Then I think of the little boy who had brought so much happiness into my world, how together we laughed, how many nights I cried unbeknown to this child, how many nights I worried about our future but the next day, I knew that GOD was at our side and would see us through. YES HE DID! Now I have lost that little boy and I like mothers who have lost their sons, must "cling to the memories" that made all sacrifices worthwhile.

Yes, I know I lost my son, know that I have been denounced as a mother, know that hatred was left in this house by you and your wife. You two cannot even call me Lynn, has hatred dug so deep into the heart of a young man who once wanted to place his life as a priest helping people like myself who call on Pastors for mental health? And if as many people have told me, that it is not "your doing", (which I do not believe), how can you allow anyone to murder your own mother?

Murder your mother? Yes every bit of that. Although you and Kathy murdered Lynn Simmons, your mother, the children's grandmother, a new person has erupted from this broken down woman. In the following doctor's orders, I have been instructed to "forget Andy Acciaioli, forget Kathy Rocchio and forget the two innocent babies."

Well, I cannot find it too difficult to forget Kathy, she has been very instrumental in breaking up our family, you Andrew Acciaioli have placed me against the stake and burned me alive, so in time I will forget the little boy I loved and cared for into manhood, but Kristen – how do I go about forgetting an innocent little girl whom I was forced to see "by appointment"? The little girl who has to look at me for a few minutes, hear me speak to be reminded that I am her grandmother. How can I forget this innocent baby who has been used as a tool to keep you away? Baby Matthew? Oh GOD, I wish I had gotten to know him, but he too was taken away and KEPT AWAY so he would not know his grandmother.

It took a long time for me to believe the doctor, he told me, "Lynn, you have got to believe that your son does not want to have anything to do with you and his wife is doing all to keep you away from the babies?"

Well it did take me a long time to digest this, in fact it took one whole year and though I am still suffering I have got to believe that "Time heals all wounds" and mine too will be healed period.

I had been advised to "clear all the hatred, (if any), by telling all who have hurt me what they have done but this past year drained too much energy from me and I must be strong for the sake of my family? Oh no, I do not have a family, but I must for the sake of the business.

Everything is changing for the better. From a penniless hungry person who was forced to live in the basement because she had to give up her apartment for money to survive, to this new person who one year ago today wanted to die and now, is finding out what the people really are the people whom she gave her all to. The new Lynn Simmons, has had a rough time but has come a long way.

...

Mom provided an introduction to one of our new neighbors when she left the above letter in an envelope with their address right in their mailbox. No name, just the address. No doubt Mom wrote down the address while at our house the night before, either before or after dining with us. Thinking the unmailed letter was meant for her or her husband, our neighbor opened the envelope and found Mom's hate letter.

Embarrassed, I gave her a thumbnail view of my mom. She more than understood. As a matter of fact she proceeded to tell us she can barely stand to be in the same room with her mother-in-law for all the hateful actions she pulled during the 42 years of her marriage. In the end, Mom's letter not only forced a meeting with our new neighbors, but it also began a friendship that lasted long after we moved out of our starter, three-toned safe haven into one with more room across the city.

To recap:

Tuesday – May 21st: Mom called me at our Hartley Tours office demanding my GANBC Realty 50% ownership stock certificate back.

Wednesday – May 22nd: Mom stopped by to visit with Kathy and the kids in the afternoon and stayed for dinner.

Thursday – May 23rd: Mom's May 21st threatening letter arrived at my office.

Friday – May 24th: Mom's May 22nd letter was placed in our neighbor's mailbox.

In mid-June a rattled senior citizen tour group leader came to our office. It seems that Mom was soliciting her people at their senior citizen apartment complex and not going through her as the travel coordinator. Mom got their names and telephone numbers when they were on a bus she escorted to Hickey's the previous summer on a tour promoted by this same group leader. I could understand and sympathize about how rotten it was of Mom to steal her customers, but there was really nothing I could do.

When she produced a single sheet of paper filled with trips by "Lynn Simmons Tours," I gave it a quick glance and noticed it was almost identical to ours except for different dates. Then I noticed that under "Lynn Simmons Tours" was the line: "Formerly Great Age/Hartley Tours."

A few photocopies were made and the tour group leader, appeased, went home. I grabbed a copy and went to visit Miss Lynn, who failed to see anything wrong with giving the impression that Lynn Simmons Tours was the surviving tour operator of Great Age/Hartley. In her tangled logic, she felt justified in using my registered trademarks, even though she was never affiliated with Hartley Tours in any way. I tried to use a rational approach, explaining that while it was okay to say that she was personally "formerly with Great Age," she could not say her new business was. This proved to be a waste of words; she did not want to hear it. In her mind, Lynn Simmons Tours rose from the ashes of Great Age and Hartley Tours.

I left convinced there was no way to get through to my mom, while at the same time I tried to figure out a way to protect our trademarks from being smirched by her sloppy business and sales techniques: Over promising and under delivering. When I got back to the office, I contacted our trademark attorney and explained the situation. He felt as though we should sue or at least threaten to sue her by sending a letter ordering Mom to immediately cease using our registered trademarks. I opted for the letter.

In response to the letter, Mom sent a five page poison pen letter detailing how "rotten to the core" I was for leaving her penniless - penniless? - with the only thing being left to her was her good name. Now I wanted that, too. Not a word was mentioned about using our trademarks without permission.

Mom alludes to an imagined court case over her use of the Hartley trademark in a letter I've included in Chapter 20. In her mind, my trademark attorney – whom she never met – was a dear friend of hers, and he told her that he was sure she could win the trademark case against Hartley (me, her son). Which is exactly what happened! Miss Lynn's imaginary state judge found Miss Lynn did nothing wrong with the unauthorized use of our federally registered trademarks, and that she could continue to use them. I had no idea that a fictionalized state judge had jurisdiction over a federal matter.

This was getting out-of-control nutty. I was once again dragged into Mom's web of delusion.

Maureen thought it would be best to ignore her and concentrate on Hartley Tours.

She was right. Over the next six months, we grew from our Reservoir Avenue location to seven additional offices: 4 in Massachusetts, 2 in Rhode Island and 1 in Connecticut.

Although I was made aware that Mom was taunting me in the columns she wrote on her single page of trip offerings, I paid it no heed. One column dealt with her son suing her so he could use her "good name." Another dealt with how her son had stolen her first *thriving* travel company, GANBC, from her. Still another dealt with her rights as a grandmother, stating her intention to sue both Kathy and me for custody of our children due to our being *unfit* parents.

Our *Great News* newspaper was now being mailed out to 105,000 Great Age members monthly. The printer of our newspaper made a courtesy call to tell me that Miss Lynn contacted him about printing 1,000 copies of her new newspaper *Sunrise News* to promote her tours. I told him to go for it as it would not bother us in any way. Besides why should he lose the business? Mom would only go to one of his competitors.

A week or two later a copy of *Sunrise News* landed on my desk. On its front page was a photograph we had given Mom of our two children. And their full names. And specifying that they currently lived in Warwick, RI. This during a time of newspaper articles and news stories about children being kidnapped, a time when the public was becoming more educated about pedophilia, and a time when parents were teaching their children to be cautious with adults.

Maureen called Kathy to alert her to the latest Miss Lynn salvo and to tell her I had left the office borderline ballistic. As soon as I got home, Kathy and our children met me at the door, all of them wearing their pajamas. The kids were excited because, "Daddy, it's pancake night! You have to change into your pj's right now!"

Later that night, after our pancakes and sausages were eaten and our children had been put to bed, Kathy and I discussed the best way to handle my mother. My recommendations were a restraining order, lawsuit, even a resumption of the medieval rack. As usual Kathy's suggestion was the best: Do nothing, do not respond, and go on as though it doesn't bother us.

The next morning I picked up the copy of *Sunrise News* from my desk. As I glanced at my children's faces before tossing it away, something hit me, and I fished the paper out of my wastebasket to read the legend under the paper's title: "Over 150,000 members served."

I called Maureen into my office, gave her the paper and asked her if she noticed anything. Just your kids' picture, she responded. Under the name *Sunrise News,* I said. She read the 150,000 members part and we both started laughing, because we knew mom's press run was for 1,000 copies. This statement was not only a lie but a slam at *Great News* with a postal audited circulation of 105,000 copies. As Maureen left the office she said "We'd better take it up a notch, Andy. Miss Lynn's already over 150,000 members and we've only got 105,000."

I took Kathy's advice and did not react to the way Mom put our kids' picture (and names and hometown) on her front page. Nor did I respond to the other ugly postings about her evil son and his wife. I threw myself completely into the business and by November two more franchised and three more company-owned Hartley locations were added.

It was around this time we discovered that Mom was calling the same Atlantic City hotels used by Hartley and demanding they provide Lynn Simmons Tours with room blocks (at Hartley's room rate) or risk having Hartley Tours cancel its business with them. One manager of a chain of AC hotels who knew about the relationship between Lynn Simmons Tours (mom) and Hartley

Tours (me) called and said, "Andy, you're going to have to learn to control your mother."

My response: "Any suggestions?"

In November, Mom called me out of the blue and said she had received an offer on The Big House. Having fallen victim to similar phony-baloney telephone calls before, I asked for the name of the realtor making the offer and called him. He was legit. Though low, the offer turned out to be valid. We determined a timetable for closing and moving out. The realtor handled submitting a sales agreement and deposit to our attorney.

At the closing the purchaser tried to squeeze an extra couple of thousand dollars out of us. Mom rose from her chair and said the sale was off. I whispered: $797 monthly gas heating bills and she sat back down. We graciously acquiesced.

Prior to the closing, I instructed our attorney to draw up a purchase agreement whereby GANBC REALTY CORP. would purchase my 50% share of the house for $1 thereby giving Mom 100% of the proceeds of the sale, including my original deposit on the property. Once this agreement was signed, the deal was closed and someone else could call The Big House (and its expenses) home. Come to think of it, I never got my buck.

Also prior to the closing, Mom decided to shut down Lynn Simmons Tours. Although her business was extremely successful, she said, she wanted to move to the warm climate of Florida. Behind the scenes I was told by a bus company they had to stop taking her bus reservations because she canceled too many of her charters at the last minute, leaving a bus sitting in their bus yard when it could have been on the road for someone else.

Mom left for Florida after Christmas.

For the foreseeable future, there would be no more punch in the gut surprise pictures or poison postings about us published in her *Sunrise News*. The Hartley business continued its growth spurt and rapidly expanded: 22 offices (6 franchised and 16 company-owned), a bus operation with a fleet of 21 deluxe motor coaches, and a staff exceeding 130 to keep everything rolling smoothly.

In those days 800 lines were known as Wide Area Telephone Service or WATS lines. Because of their novelty, the rates charged by AT&T, the only game in town, were exorbitant: $1.10 per minute of usage during the day and $.68 per minute of usage at night. Our two incoming WATS lines were restricted to escorts and drivers calling in from the road in the event of an emergency and were answered by our dispatch department.

Mom would call in using one of these lines at least once a week, sometimes more, to chat with Maureen or other staffers she knew. These conversations would last anywhere from a half hour to an hour or more. Rarely would she ask to speak to me, preferring to spend her time (and my WATS line money) listening to the latest Hartley gossip. The only times I went berserk were when one of our WATS lines was handling a bus related problem while our second line was tied up by Mom. If another bus or tour guide ran into trouble, after trying both WATS lines they would have to use one of our reservation lines, thereby delaying our response time.

After six months of enjoying the St. Petersburg beaches, Mom got bored and decided to return to the travel business. No longer wanting to be on the road as a tour escort, she sought a tour operations position with Tampa area tour operators and eventually secured a job. Outside of her glowing descriptions to me of the outstanding job she was doing, I had no way to verify if this was true or not. For her sake I hoped it was true but knew from her past...

Most holidays she would fly home to Rhode Island to play fun Nana with our three children. (For those keeping count, we had another son, Michael, while Mom was in Florida.) Of course, she didn't hesitate to share her child rearing techniques with Kathy and me. We actually didn't have a problem with this; it was only a grandparent being a grandparent.

The visits were tolerable because they had a beginning, an end and a return flight to Florida. Followed by months of peace throughout the land.

Until...

13. She's Baaaack

"Andy, WATS 1. It's Miss Lynn. Andy, WATS 1."

"Hello?"

"Just calling to tell you that I'm leaving Florida the end of the week to come home."

I hung up, flashbacks of life with Mom whizzed through my mind: Childhood, adult, business. In somewhat of a daze, I went into Maureen's office and plopped in a chair.

"Not a good conversation, I take it." Maureen said. All I could muster was: "She's coming back."

"Well, that's not such a bad thing, Andy. At least it'll free up one of our WATS lines." Maureen's attempt at humor didn't help.

The main office for both our bus and tour operations was in a two-story building located alongside our bus maintenance facility and lengthy bus yard. About a week after the call, some woman barged by our receptionist and strolled through the offices - like she owned the place because in her mind, she did - and then proceeded up the stairs to my office. "Hi, Mom, welcome back to Rhode Island."

While driving back she said she had a lot of ideas. One can only imagine how many ideas would flow over 1,300 miles. She was going to rekindle her former tour business. Hm. I wonder which one. And all she would need is a desk somewhere in our main office. Absolutely not, I piped in, we do not allow the public on our premises due to the constant flow of buses and chances of injury. Her pitch continued: She could always meet people interested in booking her tours in our reception area. Absolutely not. In a fallback position, she would settle for a desk in our Cranston office (our busiest office). Absolutely not.

Not getting what she wanted, what she felt entitled to, she left in a huff threatening, "I'll find my own place and I'll show you."

Yup, she's baaaaaaaaaaaaaaaack.

Through the travel grapevine we learned Mom had secured desk space for her "Simmons Tours" within a travel agency. Kind of like déjà vu to her GANBC and Aylsworth Travel deal. Shortly thereafter a new edition of *Sunrise News* hit the streets, (more accurately the senior citizen centers). This one carried a large front page picture of our three children taken at Christmas. And, of course, *Sunrise News* would not be complete without a column dripping with venom aimed at her atrocious son. Especially now that he was refusing to give his own mother a little space to sell Simmons Tours in his spacious Hartley Tours building. The bastard.

To be perfectly honest, beyond looking at the picture of my children on the front cover, I never turned the page to read any of the paper's contents. We were now up to 50 buses a week going to Atlantic City plus other buses to many other destinations, as well as a full roster of day trips. I had neither the time nor the interest to enter Miss Lynn's Alternate Reality.

Maureen gave me the one sentence summary of Mom's column. And, I'm pretty sure Maureen was the one to add, "The bastard."

Same old Lynn, same old tactics: Chase our Hartley Tours group leaders to switch their business to her Simmons Tours which were priced below ours regardless of her loss. She would tell senior groups we were taking advantage of them by pricing our one day tours $3-$5 higher than hers.

For example she would sell one of our $30 Hartley Tours for $25 yielding a $3 commission and a $2 loss to her on each of these tours she sold. I would guess to Mom's convoluted way of thinking, she thought she would make up this loss by volume. Or maybe she thought she could eventually put me, her only child, out of business.

Next I heard a new column had been added to her *Sunrise News,* entitled "Letters to Miss Lynn, in which Mom would answer questions submitted to her by anonymous senders (herself). One such question was from "Sorrowful Grandmother" who was in a quandary wondering what she should do as her son and daughter-in-law were telling their children (1 girl and 2 boys...hmm seems vaguely familiar) lies about her, causing the children to not love her. One could only wonder who "Sorrowful Grandmother" was.

Miss Lynn responded to Sorrowful by writing that if she was in Sorrowful's shoes, she would get the state involved to remove the children from their present hateful environment and place them in a loving foster home. When I told Kathy about "Sorrowful Grandmother" (a/k/a Mom) she was confused: "This can't be the same Nana we and the kids get together with at some point every weekend."

Former Lynn Simmon's Tours' group leaders had not forgotten their previous experience(s) with Mom. Most of them weren't fooled by the new company name; new business, same Miss Lynn.

Occasionally she would pick-up a new group, which had never undergone The Miss Lynn Experience. Once they decided on a destination, Mom would package the hotel, restaurants and attractions and then call Ernie in our bus operations to charter one of our buses. Before he would confirm her request, he would run it by me, because she was establishing a habit of never paying us for tours booked or buses chartered (rented). Outside of our peak periods when we would have to charter buses from other bus operators to handle our own volume, I would let her use one of our buses.

One time, the Connecticut state police had set up a routine inspection area along route 95 to randomly spot check trucks and buses. Most vehicles were waved right through without stopping. Our bus with Mom and her group, returning from a Washington, DC tour, was one of the few stopped for a complete vehicle inspection and to make sure all documentation was up-to-date, including driver's logs, bus registration, insurance coverage and a valid Connecticut fuel sticker.

As soon as the bus door opened and the officer got ready to board, Miss Lynn jumped off the bus she had chartered from us and immediately got in his face about how unfair it was to stop *her* busload of seniors. Her passengers were exhausted after their long trip and wanted to get home. Why didn't he stop any of the other buses instead? She then threatened him, saying that unless he let them continue, she was going to call her politically connected friends in Connecticut who would let him have it but good.

The trooper let Mom run on until he got tired of listening to her and rapped on the by now closed bus door and instructed our driver, Mike, to follow his squad car. Mike, our best driver, complied and followed the police car to the state police barracks nearby. Once there, our bus was impounded and Mike was placed in a cell to prevent him from driving off. An incensed Miss Lynn was now chewing out anyone within hearing distance wearing a uniform, including the commander of the barracks.

"Sorry to disturb you at home, boss, but I got a call about ten minutes ago from the state police barracks in Westbrook,

Connecticut. Our bus has been impounded and Mike is in jail. Bill is on his way in to take a bus from the yard to drive down and rescue the passengers. I'm driving down to handle getting Mike out and our bus home."

"Ernie, tell me it wasn't my mother's bus."

"It was her bus and from what the statie just told me, boss, your mother was going to be thrown in the cell next to Mike's, but the passengers were screaming to leave her alone."

Pause.

"Thanks, Ernie. Please keep me posted."

Simmons Tours was never again allowed to charter another bus from us, which turned out to be not much of a problem since Mom couldn't fill a bus with 48 passengers on her own.

Mom would call our branch office closest to her to book individual reservations, always attempting to muscle our office associates into giving her more than our standard travel agency commission by using the old, "I'm Miss Lynn, Andy's mother" line. Depending on the tour, they would usually bump up her commission by a couple of percentage points.

I use to dread these calls from the manager of our branch office where Mom would book her passengers: "Andy, I've got your mom on hold. She booked 6 people on Saturday's whale watching tour but wants me to give her a comp so she can go too."

I would always clear the comp for Mom in spite of her not fulfilling our "fill 23 seats and you go free" requirement. Trust me, taking the $30 - $50 hit was a lot easier than listening to how bad I was to my own mother for thirty minutes or seeing a 6PM news report on how Ungrateful Son refuses to comp Sorrowful Mother.

Regrettably, I allowed this on one of our Atlantic City trips when she wanted to accompany her group of 12 for free. The tour escort on Mom's bus contacted Maureen when she returned and told her, "...all was going fine until just after the dinner stop on our way home when Andy's mother proceeded to pass out her Simmons Tours business cards, telling our passengers her Atlantic City trips were priced much lower than Hartley's because she did not have anywhere near Hartley's overhead."

I spoke with the escort to confirm her conversation with Maureen. Reviewing the passenger list for that trip, I noticed a few passenger names I recognized as having traveled with us since our basement tour operation days and called them. They verified the story, but knowing Miss Lynn was my mom did not want to report her to the office, fearing Miss Lynn would find out and let loose her retaliatory wrath on them.

I left my office and within minutes I was standing in front of her desk. I asked her point blank why she hated me, my wife and children. She said I was being ridiculous; she didn't hate her own grandchildren. Then I asked her why she continuously tried to take food out of our mouths, when all I have ever done since being forced into the travel business when she bankrupted GANBC was to make sure there was always food in hers. She feigned ignorance. I gave her the Simmons Tours business card one of the passengers had given to our escort the previous night and said her behavior was reprehensible. She claimed our escort was lying, she did no such thing.

When I told her I had gotten confirmation from other passengers, she of course wanted their names in order to confront the liars. I told her the party was over and she would no longer be allowed to be a passenger, paid or otherwise, on any further trips. Her parting blow was she was doing me a favor by putting her passengers on my buses but now she would show me and book them with my competition.

As I left I thought, what is it that makes her treat her own child like this over money? Putting parental love aside, something has to be severely broken to lack a sense of what is morally right or wrong, to lack a conscience.

Regardless of all Mom's viciously false statements against us and despite her blatant attempt to steal my customers and harm my company, Kathy insisted we maintain the family relationship between our family and the children's nana. This was more difficult for me than any obstruction I had ever encountered in salvaging her GANBC business for her or building my own.

How could you play gladiator all week fending off personal and family attacks from this woman and then sit down and play nice at a Sunday meal? Especially knowing you were eating across from a loaded grenade which would in all probability explode before too long?

Kathy and I never spoke about my mother or her behavior in front of our kids. We didn't have to. Children are far more perceptive than we think. They saw through their nana's façade to the insincere and hurtful woman who relentlessly tormented their mother and father – and later, they as well - during forced Nana visits.

As our children grew older, they would refuse to go to Mom's with us unless it was a holiday. Even those festive visits turned out to be just another opportunity for Mom to nag them: How come you never visit? Doesn't your phone work? How come you never call me? Did your parents tell you any stories about me?

Needless to say, our children stopped visiting altogether. And rarely called her.

One Hartley rule was all of our tours had to be one-hundred percent paid for one month before the tour's departure. There were no exceptions. If any travel agent, group leader or individual passenger failed to comply, the seats or full buses we were holding for them were released back into our available inventory.

Mom constantly broke our payment policy by (once again) playing the "I'm Andy's mother" card. The Hartley branch office manager where we set up Mom's business account with Hartley Tours contacted me out of desperation, fearful that all of Mom's tour non-payments would affect her own sales incentive pay. It seems Mom was into our company for a lot of money and was due to leave for a 3 day/2 night Atlantic City tour within a couple of days. Since the office had not received payment or a passenger list our staffer sought my intervention.

I called Mom to get an update and told her the office had yet to receive payment. She told me her bus was sold out (48 passengers) and she was waiting for a few passenger payments that afternoon before her accountant would issue a check to Hartley. Accountant? Could that be Frisky the cat? I knew she didn't have any employees. Or, silly me, maybe David was now a CPA. Before she ended the call, Mom promised to deliver the passenger list and payment in full to our branch office later that day.

At the close of business no Miss Lynn, no payment, no passenger list and no answer at Simmons Tours. The Hartley branch manager called me in panic mode. I told her not to worry, I would handle my mother but in the future do not accept any reservations from Simmons Tours unless I personally reopen her account.

I tried calling her office line, no one picked-up. She did not pick-up her home phone but it did go to her answering machine. My message was brief: "Mom, it's me. It's now 5:25 Wednesday. If I don't hear from you by 6, I'll assume your bus scheduled to depart on Friday is canceled."

A few minutes later, a raspy-voiced Mom called me back. "You've got some nerve, junior, treating your own mother like this."

I reminded her of her promise to go to the office with a passenger list and payment in full. Her response, "That's just like you; you're an animal like your father. I'm dying and you want me to drive."

I explained that had she followed the rules, she wouldn't have to get out of her deathbed now to do what she should have done a month ago. For the record, my mother had been dying since I was 5 or 6. After so many years one becomes desensitized to the dying diva routine.

"If you cancel my bus, I'm going to sue. Think of how that's going to embarrass you, a mother suing her own big shot son. Then you watch when the word gets out, your Hartley Tours will be in the sewer where it belongs."

I told her that at this late date, having already guaranteed payment for her bus' 25 Atlantic City hotel rooms, Hartley would be eating the entire cost. However, by canceling the bus, at least I wouldn't have to eat the transportation cost, as well.

As for suing me? I was quite sure the judge would be interested to see the Hartley Tours printout of the extensive number of trips sold by the mother and never paid for by the mother, because the mother pocketed the cash, instead.

"I'll be there, first thing in the morning. Don't you dare cancel my goddamn bus." Slam.

She was there first thing in the morning, if your morning starts at 4:30 in the afternoon. Telling our manager she was in a hurry, she handed her a sealed envelope. Inside were the names of 27 passengers (instead of 48, which meant we would be taking a hit on transpiration related expenses) and 14 rooms paid for instead of 25 (which meant we would also be taking a bath on the 11 unoccupied rooms we had guaranteed to fill).

Upon first hearing of this passenger shortfall, my impulse was to pick-up the phone and go all crazy pants. Then I realized this was it. Simmons Tours was officially shut off from ever booking another Hartley Tour. Period. End of story.

As it turned out it wasn't quite the end of this story: The following Wednesday, accounting notified me that one of our travel agency customers had given us a rubber check.

The name on the check? Simmons Tours.

14. Kids Behaving Badly

It didn't take very long before Mom said she was closing Simmons Tours because it had grown to be so successful she had no time for herself. Translation: No bus company (including mine), hotel, restaurant or popular attraction would work with Simmons Tours because of her high last minute cancel rate and/or non-payment. In the end, Hartley was left with more than $30,000 (around $70,000 today) in worthless Simmons Tours account receivables.

When I asked her what she was going to do, she said she wanted to take some time off, maybe go down to Florida and visit her friends Pat and Maria. After she returned she would seek part-time work in a tour operator's office, maybe with Collette Tours. (Collette Tours, based in Pawtucket, RI was – and still is – a huge operation compared to Hartley Tours. Although Collette grew primarily from the motor coach tour business, their largest expansion came from air tours.) I said, "When you see Dan [Sullivan, owner of Collette Tours], give him my regards"

Her departure and a few happy, stress-free and productive months followed, allowing me to laser-focus my complete attention on Hartley Tours and our Andrews Transportation bus company.

It couldn't last, of course.

A major airline working with an offshore casino was eager to tap into our large Atlantic City gambling market. As I was meeting with one of the airline's representatives, I heard a commotion downstairs followed by footsteps climbing the stairs and coming down the hall to my office.

My closed office door swung open and there stood Miss Lynn with her brother, my Uncle Ernie, following in her wake. Our harried receptionist, Mary, who had obviously tried to stop them from steam rolling their way through our offices unannounced, stood nervously behind them.

I told Mary not to worry, that only an Act of God - and even that's questionable - could have stopped my mother, and she left the office, closing the door behind her.

Mom disingenuously introduced herself to the airline rep as, "I'm Miss Lynn. I started Hartley Tours many years ago. Andy is my son." Started Hartley Tours? The mind, it boggles.

Not to be outdone by his sister, Uncle Ernie piped in, "I'm Rusty's Uncle Ernie." Rusty. Did I just hear Rusty? Of course.

After explaining the obvious, that there was a meeting going on, I suggested they grab a coffee in our downstairs break room and I would see them after my meeting. They agreed, and as Mom swept out of the office, she said over her shoulder, "Don't you two be long, because I'm a very busy woman and have lots of things to do today."

While my mind was still frantically trying to come up with some sort of reasonable explanation, the airline rep said, "Your mom seems like a force to be reckoned with."

My only response: "You have no idea."

The meeting concluded on a positive note. As I ushered my visitor down the stairs to the reception area, we passed the break room. Please don't let her see us, please don't let...

"You'd better treat my son right or else you'll have his mommy to contend with." Mommy. Great. Terrific.

By the time I returned to the break room I was livid and slammed the door behind me.

MOM: You seem to be upset.

ME: Who does that?

MOM: Does what?

ME: Barges in to someone's office and interrupts a meeting vital to the future of my business?

MOM: See, Ernie, that's the thanks we get for stopping by to say hello. Andrew, we will never stop by to see you again.

ME: Great.

MOM: Don't you want to know why we stopped by?

ME: No.

MOM: While I was away, my friend Marge, who escorts for you, you know Marge.

ME: I know Marge.

MOM: Marge said you're always in desperate need of tour escorts with so many buses going out. And I thought instead of our going to work for Collette, Uncle Ernie and I could be escorts on your buses.

ME: No. No. And hell no. You refuse to follow directions. You are incapable of following directions.

MOM (*getting up to leave*): If you change your mind, you can call us if you need us. Come on, Ernie.

UNCLE: Give us another chance. You know my passengers have a lot of fun.

ME: Believe me, I know from personal experience, the drag bar in Miami, you nearly OD'd me on sangria in Torromolimos. You're a barrel of laughs.

They left and I resolved to send a tour out escort less rather than put either one of them on any tour of mine.

Because it was the Christmas holiday season, we had a number of multi-day tours to special destinations with unique, spectacular holiday displays. In addition, we were stretched to capacity with our buses and touring staff covering New York City shopping and Radio City Music Hall tours.

In addition to the buses leaving daily, we were walloped with reservations on weekends. It wasn't unusual for us to send 12 – 14 buses to New York on Saturdays and Sundays.

On the Friday night following my close encounter with the dynamic duo of Miss Lynn and Uncle Ernie, my tour operations manager came into my office around 10:30PM. She looked depleted of every last ounce of energy she had carried into her office fourteen and a half hours ago. Every escort we had – or ever had – was either out on tour, on their way home from a tour, going out on tour the next morning or sick. Of the nineteen departures leaving in a matter of hours, we had three New York buses still without escorts.

"I know I'm going to regret this. Call my mother and Uncle Ernie. Give them a single pick-up area in order for them not to screw it up. Leave their paperwork in the dispatch office; I'll give it to them in the morning." Okay, that's two, what about the third, she asked me. "You're gonna love New York this time of year. I'll handle tour operations with dispatch." Problem solved.

Driving home to catch a few hours of sleep, I thought, what the hell did I just do? Instead of three problems – being down three escorts - I now potentially have two busloads of 96 ticked off passengers angry about Mom and Uncle Ernie. Too late and too exhausted to do anything about it now.

Around 4 the next morning, bearing gifts of Dunkin Donuts coffee and a couple dozen donuts, I turned onto Route 146. My early-departing buses started passing me, with their blazing front marquees reading "Hartley Tours," and their distinctive white on green huge exterior bus lettering: "Andrews." It always excited me to see multiple buses leaving.

It's gonna be a great day! No, Andy, no it's not. It's gonna be a Mom and Uncle Ernie day.

When I arrived at our office, Ernie, our bus operations manager, said everything was running smoothly so far. Operative words "so far". Wait until the dynamic duo arrives.

Within the hour that "smoothly so far" vanished along with most of the donuts, and the phones started ringing. A group leader of a full bus going to Radio City from the Boston area promised about half of her passengers a special pick-up twenty miles north of where her bus was supposed to have been fully loaded. Ordinarily this would not be a major problem, but this particular bus was ticketed for a late morning Radio City performance. Adding an additional hour to the trip could make them late for the show.

This call was the first of many. There were passengers assigned to one pick-up area showing up at another, people bringing friends with them, assuming they could pay the tour price to the escort and squeeze their friends on a sold out bus, passengers wanting to hold the bus for family or friends who had called them earlier to ask them to tell the escort they would only be 15 or 20 minutes late…

"Knock, knock." With the phone hermetically sealed to my ear, I turned and nodded to Mom.

"Listen I don't want to bother you but I need bingo cards."

I motioned for her to go into the escorts' supply closet and take whatever she needed.

"I was thinking since Ernie and I are going to the Warwick Park 'n Ride for our pickups, I'll take his paperwork with me so he can meet his bus out there instead of having to drive all the way here."

Muffling the phone, attempting to "serenity now" myself, I informed Mom that this was not how we operated. All escorts report to the yard where we are able to do a visual that a bus is departing with the assigned driver and the scheduled tour escort.

"But I already told your uncle to meet the bus in Warwick."

SERENITY NOW. "Call him up and tell him that's not how we operate. All escorts leave from the yard."

A little later, Uncle Ernie arrived in time to board his bus. Walking back to the dispatch office to say hello, he was intercepted by Mom: "Don't bother, my son is ornery."

Visual: She's gone. Visual: He's gone.

It's gonna be a great day.

With so many buses heading to New York from Hartley Tours and other bus companies in the area, it was essential to make breakfast reservations months in advance, and our bus arrivals had to be staggered. You couldn't just pull up to a restaurant and request a table for 50.

Buses leaving from Lowell, MA, down through Greater Boston would be our furthest and earliest pick-up areas. They would be sent to the closest restaurant over the Connecticut state line capable of handling a large crowd quickly. In this case we were sending them to 76 Truck Stop (now called T/A New Haven), alongside route 95 at Exit 56. Buses departing from southern Massachusetts or Rhode Island were scheduled to go to restaurants located fifteen minutes further down 95 at Exit 42. Breakfast stops were assigned and pre-designated for each bus.

All tour escorts knew exactly where their breakfast reservations were. It was noted on their paperwork. Did Miss Lynn follow tour operations' instructions and take her bus to her designated restaurant at Exit 42? Everybody together now: Not a chance.

She smashed the flow of staggered buses into smithereens by heading to 76 Truck Stop, which was already feeding four of our buses (200 passengers). Once she arrived, she ignored the four empty Hartley buses parked in front and the fact that 76 Truck Stop was filled to capacity by ordering her passengers off the bus. Once in the restaurant where they clogged the aisles, Miss Lynn instructed them to take any available seat, anywhere in the restaurant as soon as it was vacated by a fellow Hartley passenger (from one of the other buses).

Let me try to explain why this is wrong:

Restaurants handling multiple buses seat each bus in a specific section. This makes it easier for their wait staff to identify which orders have to be processed first for Bus 1, second for Bus 2, and so on. Once you scatter the passengers from Miss Lynn's bus throughout the restaurant, it puts an immediate strain on the wait staff's ability to prioritize and slows up the ordering process, not just for Miss Lynn's bus, but for ALL the other buses.

A second problem is created for newly arriving buses when Miss Lynn's passengers start sitting all over the restaurant. The arriving buses are now forced to mix their passengers in with Miss Lynn's scattered passengers. This makes it impossible for the wait staff to prioritize and really slows things down, especially for the passengers already running late for their scheduled late morning Radio City performance.

As a result the later buses scheduled to stop for breakfast at 76 have to be waved away because the backup wait is too long, and the wait staff (and kitchen) are finding it difficult to manage the chaos.

Pandemonium soon followed.

Escorts and drivers began calling in screaming, no doubt because their passengers were screaming at them. Since the drivers now anticipated an hour's delay getting to New York, I extended their departure from the city from 7PM to 8PM, even knowing the ramifications: Passengers' families or friends at the pick-up areas would have to wait an hour before our buses arrived back home.

The problem for us: Our coordinated turn around schedule of getting returning New York buses serviced (interiors cleaned, exteriors washed, lavs dumped and tanks fueled) for the next morning's departures would be impossible to meet. This was going to affect tomorrow's schedule, causing passenger pick-up delays.

Early Monday morning before our offices opened, a fax was sent to each Hartley branch manager explaining the problem at the breakfast stop that caused a delay in Saturday's New York City arrivals. Office staffs were instructed to apologize to all of our passengers for the inconvenience and to tell them that they would receive 10% off their next Hartley Tour.

"It's gonna be a great day?" Not so much.

When Mom arrived at the office late Monday morning to turn in her paperwork from Saturday, tour operations informed her that I wanted to see her. She walked into my office with an upbeat "la-

la-la everything is wonderful" persona, and I asked her why she didn't go to the breakfast restaurant specified on her paperwork.

"I was hungry and my people were hungry. What's the problem?"

I was boiling on the inside but stone cold on the outside: "The problem? Well, there were four buses already eating at 76, six other buses were staggered to arrive at various times as the other four buses departed. Then Miss Lynn decides to show up and destroys our schedule because she was hungry. This caused turmoil at the restaurant and delays for hundreds of my other passengers going to New York. The angry phone calls started bright and early this morning, and I will be taking God only knows how much of a financial hit with my having to give all passengers on the affected buses 10% off on a future trip."

Miss Lynn was unmoved. In fact, she was angry. "Don't crab at me. I was only trying to keep your passengers happy."

When she stormed out of my office, I couldn't resist calling down the stairway after her: "Do me a favor, go to Collette."

Most people receive Christmas Cards or Christmas Newsletters at Christmas time. I got an acerbic letter from Mom stating, "Everyone" at my main office was calling her to express their shock and sorrow over "the way you treated me." The piece de resistance? All of them, each and every one, want to work for Simmons Tours as soon as she gets it going again. I'm sure they do, Mom, I'm sure they do. They probably can't wait to get paid with subject-to-change Miss Lynn's points.

This missive a few days before Christmas pushed me into my kid's column: I never wanted to see or in any way communicate with "Nana" ever again. Kathy worked me over relentlessly short of water boarding: Regardless of your mom's actions, she's still your mother and you're still her only child.

The day before Christmas, Kathy and I stopped by Mom's place to exchange gifts, because a house full of relatives was expected Christmas Day and we wanted to give Mom time to open all of her gifts with us. Our reception was frigid and grew colder as the minutes passed. Mom methodically opened the gifts we bought her with snippy comments like, "Kathy I thought you would know by now my tops are medium and not large." Doubtful Mom fit into a medium since her teen years, but I digress.

Without looking, Mom reached under the tree, grabbed the first gift that came to hand, and gave it to me. "This was very expensive, open it.

Shiny gold elf slippers, with curled toes. In a size too small even for our youngest son's feet. Top of my Christmas list. Mom said Kathy's gift was on order. Must be some gift; it's decades later and it still remains undelivered. Since her grandchildren did not come with us to see her, she didn't give them anything.

When I told Mom that dinner would be at three the next day, she declined because she and David had made other plans. Kathy had that *Andrew, don't go there* look on her face. Ignoring her, I said, "Bring David over to our house. After all it's Christmas. You've been talking about him for over thirty years. I would love to finally meet him."

Mom said this would not be possible. He was scheduled to leave the day after Christmas to resume command as captain of a large aircraft carrier in the Gulf. Kathy shook her head at me: *Andrew, no, no, not a word.*

"An aircraft carrier, huh? I really want to meet this guy more than ever. He's a Wall Street tycoon. He's a lawyer. He's a heart surgeon. Now he drives an aircraft carrier. He seems to have trouble holding a steady job, though. Merry Christmas, Mom."

Kathy was upset over my sarcastic comments to Mom about David, even if he wasn't an actual person. Fictional David was mentioned by Mom to Kathy on two or three occasions. I had the pleasure of "knowing" David since I was in the seventh grade, when Mom first started using him as a weapon against her string of beaus.

The next morning we called Mom to wish her a Merry Christmas.

Right after the first of the year, Mom called me at the office and said she wanted to stop by. I told her I would be in all day. When she arrived, she asked Mary to buzz me to let me know she was on her way up. Okay, what's she up to now? No unannounced surprise attack? What does she want?

Mom walked in carrying coffee and donuts. We small talked for a bit and then she asked me what was going on with the Hartley office in New Haven. I asked her what she knew about it, and she said she knew that Ray, my branch office manager, had been down there for months trying to make a go of it without success. I asked for her source, and she refused to say. I guess it didn't matter. Mom was correct: I was getting ready to close the New Haven office. It was a financial drain, and I needed Ray back in our main office coordinating all branch office activity.

I asked what she was proposing. She said she was anxious to move back to Connecticut and running the New Haven office would be a first step. After she turned the office around with her sales ability, she wanted me to give the office to her as a franchised location. "Of course, since I'm your mother, I don't expect to pay any franchise fee."

Sounded fine with me. In addition to her pay as a branch manager and receiving incentives (more money) as reasonable sales thresholds were met or surpassed, Mom would also have living expenses (hotel and food) covered. In terms of a time frame we would give it three months, until the first week of April, then review the viability of keeping Hartley/New Haven open.

Mom's training began the following week when Ray taught her the essentials of running a Hartley office. Central to our branch office operation is the ability to transmit via computer all reservations at the end of each day. Once received, they would be added to our master reservation database.

Facing that computer screen for the first time was daunting to any 50-plusser, including Mom. Many of them were afraid of making a mistake that would obliterate Peoria, Illinois. Ray told Mom not to worry about it as all reservations transmitted by someone new to the team are placed in a separate transmission file and its data checked for accuracy before it was merged into our master reservation database.

I have no doubt that Mom gave it her best effort, since her personal motive was to return to Connecticut and her business goal was to own a thriving Hartley Tours office. Unfortunately, with our April review we found the office was bleeding to the tune of ten thousand dollars a month.

Against my better business judgment, I decided to keep the office open through June. With the additional advertising dollars pumped into the dying office, the monthly losses rose to more than twelve thousand dollars.

Sadly, by the end of June we had to pull the plug. Mom returned to her Rhode Island apartment and remained bitter over my decision, claiming that all the office needed was more time. Considering we were well on our way to losing a hundred and fifty thousand dollars that year solely from the New Haven office, keeping it open made absolutely no business sense. Still Mom told some of her family and mutual friends that I shuttered *her* New Haven office just when she had it turning a profit. Although I didn't appreciate the way she was handling her disappointment, I felt the same loss. This was the first time I had to close a Hartley Tours office.

A few weeks later I called and asked Mom to meet me for lunch. We spent most of it performing a New Haven office cry-in-our-beer postmortem. It was then, during a moment of weakness, that I suggested she go back on the road as a tour escort. This would occupy her time until another Hartley office opportunity opened up in any of our four other Connecticut locations.

Mom jumped at my offer with one caveat. All of her assigned tours had to be Atlantic City runs, because she loved to play the slots. No problem, we had a ton of buses traveling there weekly.

"And I also want Uncle Ernie back on as a tour escort too."

I consented but added terms of my own:

Mom would always be assigned to a two bus move. Her bus would always be followed by a chaser bus to make sure she didn't take any detours.

The only times she and Uncle Ernie would be assigned to work the same trip would be in a three or more bus move, with Uncle Ernie in Bus 1, Mom in Bus 2, and the chaser bus in last position.

Since our Atlantic City trips are coordinated with casino greeters' schedules, Mom had to adhere to our tight arrival time constraint, leaving no room for any sort of delayed arrivals outside of weather and traffic conditions.

She agreed.

When I returned to the office, I told tour ops to include Mom and Uncle Ernie in the Atlantic City escort rotation. Bus Ops Ernie started laughing, "Great, boss, glad to hear The Kids are back."

Initially, seeing the name of one or two of The Kids on the next day's departure schedule elicited instantaneous anxiety. Over the following months, I was able to relax my guard when there were no major incidents involving Mom or Uncle Ernie, and the sight of their names didn't faze me.

As time went on, our most experienced drivers would request one of The Kids to be the tour escort on their buses, because they would receive the highest amount of passenger tips when Miss Lynn or Uncle Ernie were on board.

Looking back at it many years later, I can understand why it was a financial windfall to drive a bus with one of The Kids as your sidekick. Mom's willingness to ignore Hartley tour operational procedures amused her passengers, and they liked her assertiveness and the way she always stuck up for them (or used their presence to get her own way). Her brother, Ernie, was a great guy, always joking around and up for any of Miss Lynn's shenanigans.

By December, I had totally relaxed my guard. After all, what could be simpler than picking up your passengers at Point A in New England and delivering them to Point B, Atlantic City, New Jersey? The first time The Kids decided to change it up a little was when they decided to take a slight detour and bring their passengers to see New York City decorated for Christmas. Included in their side tour, you know between point A and B, was a stop for pictures at the famous Rockefeller Center Christmas tree.

Outside of the flagrant disregard for our company policy, this was wrong on so many levels. New York City was off our designated route. It was a Friday afternoon before Christmas with congested city drive time traffic. And apart from the liability of letting the passengers off the bus to mingle with the crowds and take pictures, their jaunt threw them off schedule by hours. Which was why their two buses were three and a half hours behind our other tour buses arriving in Atlantic City.

Because they were late, they missed their scheduled first casino stop. The hotel had to keep their bellmen on beyond their shifts to wait for them. And it gave all of us in bus and tour ops back at the main office *agita* as we chomped on Tums and wondered where in the world The Kids had had taken their hijacked buses. It was during this completely unnecessary crisis that the dispatch department started calling the tours Miss Lynn was assigned to The Miss Lynn Triangle, where buses unexpectedly vanish between Point A and Point B not unlike the disappearance of ships and aircraft traveling within the Bermuda Triangle.

Once The Kids finally arrived at the hotel, hotel greeters handed Uncle Ernie, on Bus 1, his box of enveloped room keys with passenger names and room assignments written on the outside of each envelop. A similar box of envelopes was given to Miss Lynn, who was also instructed to make sure the names on the envelopes matched the names of her passengers before handing out her room keys. She was also instructed to hold all of her passengers on her bus until everyone on Bus 1 was inside the hotel.

Uncle Ernie's bus started to unload. Did Miss Lynn wait? Not even a nanosecond, not with so many slot machines calling her name. Her bus door opened, and she stepped out followed by her passengers. Once they were all off the bus, she quickly handed each of them an enveloped room key. Without asking for a single name.

The simultaneous unloading of two buses created turmoil in the lobby. Instead of fifty people rushing to the elevators to get to their rooms, there were now one hundred, but the real fun started once the passengers were in their rooms.

Two of Miss Lynn's passengers, let's call them the Davis', arrived in their hotel room. Mrs. Davis was off to the casino while Mr. Davis was off to the bathroom. Not getting a response from his door knock, the bellman drops off Mr. and Mrs. Smiths' luggage into the Smiths' (hotel assigned) room and then leaves.

When Mr. Davis emerges from the bathroom, he discovers the luggage. Not his wife and his luggage but Mr. and Mrs. Smiths' luggage. He calls the front desk and tells them of *their* error.

A short time later a bellman picks up the Smiths' luggage. Mr. Davis scolds the bellman who does not have a clue which room Mr. Davis' luggage had been delivered to.

The front desk is experiencing extreme disarray as their room assignments - only on Miss Lynn's bus - were all wrong resulting in a lobby full of returned luggage and their having to wait for a screaming passenger to give them his/her name and room number before the bellmen could sort through the pile of suitcases and finally get it delivered to the proper room.

This routine process of getting luggage off of a bus and up to passengers' rooms was usually accomplished in a matter of minutes. Miss Lynn's bus took hours.

Some pieces of luggage didn't reach their destination room until well beyond midnight when passengers who dashed off to a casino as soon as the bus arrived finally returned to the hotel in the wee hours of the morning unknowingly passing their own luggage in the lobby. Once they arrived in their room they discovered their luggage had never been delivered. Instead a Mr. and Mrs. Davis' suitcase was sitting on their luggage stand.

You might be wondering if anything could be worse than this.

Suppose you were the Jacksons and wanted to call your longtime friends, the Smiths, to tell them you were ready to leave for dinner. You call the hotel operator and she cheerfully connects you to the Smith's room however a grumpy Mr. Davis answers because he still hasn't received his luggage. You hang up and repeatedly punch in "0" to reach that *idiot* hotel operator. She apologizes for connecting you to the wrong room, looks up the Smith's room once again from her telephone system's guest list and reconnects you.

A maniac Mr. Davis answers his phone. You quickly hang up and head down to strangle the first front desk person you can find. This is just too much: first your luggage is messed up now these incompetents can't even connect you to the Smith's room.

You get the picture.

While my other Hartley escorts frantically tried to assist the hotel in straightening out the mess, where were Calamity Lynn and Uncle Ernie? Unreachable. Playing the slots at a nearby casino.

Like Popeye, I couldn't stands no more. I didn't want Mom to even look at a passing Hartley Tours motor coach, much less ride in one.

Uncle Ernie was dealt with more lightly. We figured he had always been influenced by his sister. Without Miss Lynn to lead him astray, he'd be fine.

A month later Uncle Ernie decided to take his Atlantic City bound passengers on a side trip – he would later term it a tour within the tour - to see where Frank Sinatra was born. When he directed his driver off the Garden State Parkway, his chaser bus followed, figuring there must be a mechanical problem. They drove through Jersey Shore's Asbury Park in search of the Sinatra homestead, cruising down narrow side streets like they were driving a Mini Cooper instead of a 45 foot bus. After 30 minutes or so of aimless driving, one of the tour staffers spotted a police officer and asked for directions to the Sinatra house.

"It's about an hour north of here in Hoboken."

When Uncle Ernie returned home, like his sister, Miss Lynn, before him, he joined her in escort hell, never to walk the center aisle on any Hartley Tour bus again.

Months later with Easter weekend fast approaching, tour ops anticipated road staffing shortages. By the Wednesday before our Friday Easter weekend departures, we were down seven escorts.

"Andy, I know you're going to kill me for this," my tour operations manager said as she entered my office.

I looked up and said, "Hell, no."

She said she hadn't even told me what she'd done, yet.

I knew what she'd done, she'd called The Kids, and my answer to that was a double no-way-in-hell no. As she left the office I sarcastically added, "I'd rather get on one of those buses and escort the damn tour myself than send either of them."

Without turning around she said, "Better get packing because the way it looks you're going to be on a bus, I'm going to be on a bus, and The Kids are going to be on buses, too."

The rest of that day was spent making calls to our entire team of escorts, hoping to convince seven of them to change their minds and leave their families for Easter. I even called escorts I worked with back in the early days. No luck.

Around 7PM I visited tour ops to see how things were going. "Got a call from Donna a few minutes ago. She went to one of those walk-in ER's because she couldn't stop vomiting. Bottom line, she's got the flu and can't escort the DC tour this weekend. And now we need eight."

Feeling more desperate by the second, I barked, "Keep working on it. Maybe Donna could still do it if she takes a throw-up bucket with her."

Sometime after 10 o'clock I decided to go home. It was probably too late to get a call back from the messages I'd left on a bunch of answering machines. My tour person was still at her desk calling friends and relatives recommended by our escorts, without success.

"Let's call it a night. It's too late to be calling anyway." I hesitated for a moment before continuing, "Before you go, please call The Kids and tell them I want them both in my office by nine in the morning. Now that the decision has been made, I'm heading out to smash my car into a bridge abutment on 95. Good night."

The following morning, while in the bus garage meeting with Bus Ops Ernie, a page came over the loudspeaker, "Andy, The Kids are here."

Ernie looked at me and asked, "What did they do this time, boss?"

"Nothing yet, as far as I know. But the day's just starting, Ernie."

I led The Kids upstairs to my office and closed the door.

UNCLE: I'm really sorry about the Asbury Park thing. I was wrong.

ME: You think?

UNCLE: Definitely. Danny DeVito was born in Asbury Park not Sinatra.

ME: Danny who?

UNCLE: Danny DeVito, you know the short guy from Taxi and the movie *Throw Momma from the Train.*

ME: I hear they're making a sequel called Throw Momma under the Bus Along With Her Brother.

MOM: Me? What did I do?

ME: I don't know. Take your pick. A Christmas joy ride through New York City, screwing up passenger room assignments in Atlantic City...

MOM: That wasn't my fault. The people were tired after the long ride. I just wanted to get them settled in their rooms as quickly as possible.

ME: They were tired because our normal 5 hour drive time on that run was increased to almost 9 hours after your yuletide detour to New York City.

MOM: All I was trying to do is make YOUR passengers happy.

ME: I'm ever so grateful. But I really think it's impossible for you, either of you, to play by the rules. Tomorrow both of your buses will be sandwiched in between a lead bus and a chaser bus. There is no way in hell you will be able to exit off the route unnoticed. You'll both be on buses I had to charter from other bus companies. Their drivers have already been warned that if they deviate as much as an inch from the route, we won't pay their company for these charters.

MOM: We promise. We'll stay on the route. Honest. Right, Ernie?

UNCLE: Absolutely.

The Kids said they were in agreement, but everyone knows when dealing with children, you hope for the best but plan for the worse.

They left my office and headed down to prep for their next day's departure. Aside from picking up their trip kit, which included the passenger pick-up manifest and rooming list, they made photocopies of games to pass out to the passengers to chip away at the long drive time.

Precisely at 12:20PM, the announcement the office and garage crews were waiting for was made: "The Roach Coach is here."

I continued working for at least another twenty minutes before giving Billy, operator of the catering truck, my greasy order. Billy informed me that Miss Lynn told him I would be paying for her lunch and Uncle Ernie's. Sure. Why not?

Sitting as far away from The Kids in the break room as I could get, I still heard Uncle Ernie as he laughingly thanked me for buying lunch. I said, "No, don't thank me. It's going to be deducted from your escort pay, along with the cost of my lunch, so thank you, you guys." I never did, but I took childish pleasure in pretending I would. Geeze, maybe it runs in the family.

The next morning I drove to and waited at The Kids' Warwick passenger pick-up area to relieve my own jitters and ensure all would go smoothly, at least for their departure. While The Kids were loading their passengers, the lead bus, already fully loaded, arrived from another pick-up area. Perfect. Not only were the buses departing on time, they were actually departing a few minutes early.

This particular Easter weekend was an example of bookings exceeding our own 21 bus passenger capacity of just over 1,000 seats. We were therefore using buses hired from other bus companies.

Soon after I merged onto Route 95 heading north to our office, I saw The Kids' chaser (follow) bus. It was fully loaded from the Providence pick-up area and would be taking its position behind the other three chartered coaches in a matter of minutes.

When I finally got to the office I found everyone in good spirits. Excellent. No major missteps with any of the pick-ups. Miraculously, we were able to cajole (beg, strong arm, promise-them-anything, cry) six former and current escorts to cover the remaining six buses needing an escort.

After a while, I started to notice that the WATS lines weren't lighting up. There were no intercom announcements. No SOS's. This was bizarre, considering the number of people we were moving. And Miss Lynn and Uncle Ernie were in the escort lineup again. As most of us do when waiting for a phone call on a land line, every few minutes I felt compelled to check each WATS line to make sure it was working properly having a dial tone.

Billy's Roach Coach had come and gone over an hour ago, and still no escort emergency calls, not from Montreal bound buses, not from Washington bound buses, not even the Atlantic City buses carrying The Kids. I had been in the travel/transportation business too many years not to know it was nearly impossible for all the buses we had in motion to not have some sort of emergency be it medical or mechanical. OR The Kids behaving badly.

I glanced at the time on the phone: 2:05. Excellent. The Atlantic City bound coaches should be arriving within the next half-hour to an hour.

The premonition fell over me like a plastic shower curtain of doom. Within minutes, one of the WATS lines lit up. A few seconds later the other line started to flash. My only thought: What have The Armageddon Kids done now?

"Andy, you have a call on WATS 1. Andy, WATS 1." I grabbed the receiver and pressed the flashing button.

"Hey, Andy, I didn't know you were so desperate for business you needed to solicit my passengers while they're out on my tour."

On the phone was an out-of-state tour operator who occasionally chartered buses from us. In spite of being fierce competitors, we had an excellent rapport. I had no idea what he was talking about.

He started laughing and explained that two of our Hartley buses heading toward Atlantic City apparently gave toll attendants on the Garden State Parkway a handful of Easter egg pictures which had been colored with crayons presumably by our passengers. He went on to say that below each picture was written Happy Easter from Hartley Tours. The toll attendants were asked to give them to the next bus going through their lane. Dear God, if you're still in the smiting business, now would be the time...and The Kids would be Your smitees.

He laughed even harder when I told him who the culprits were. At the end of our conversation he said: "Watch your back, Andy. Memorial Day is right around the corner. We've already started coloring."

When I hung up, Ernie and our tour manager, having heard my page, were standing in the doorway looking glum expecting a road problem and were ready to spring into action. When I told them about The Kids latest escapade, Ernie, who had more than 50 years of bus and driver related experience, said, "I have to admit, boss, that's a new one on me."

My tour manager reminded me that Liz, a former escort had pulled the same stunt some years back on Valentine's Day. She had her passengers color in hearts and write at the bottom, "Happy Valentine's Day. With Love, Hartley Tours" and then handed them to a toll collector to pass on to the bus behind hers.

"Andy, WATS 2, Marge in Atlantic City. Andy, WATS 2."

As soon as I picked up, Marge turned me over to John, the hotel's manager, who said, "Andrew, we're in the same time zone are we not? Because down here in New Jersey it's 4PM and up in Rhode Island it's where the fuck are two of your buses?"

"Anything could have happened to delay them, traffic or weather conditions."

"How about an Easter egg hunt on the parkway south of Toms River?" he asked before erupting into laughter.

When I was able to compose myself, I weakly asked, "Can you please put Marge back on the line?"

Marge explained she was on Bus 4, the chaser bus, when it pulled into the breakdown lane behind Miss Lynn's bus and Uncle Ernie's bus. Her driver left the bus to speak with the other drivers, who said their buses had not experienced any mechanical problems but their escorts wanted to make an Easter egg hunt stop.

While Marge stood alongside her bus, she watched my uncle hop off his bus and run into the woods. Curious she walked over to my mother, who was standing outside the door of her bus, to ask what was going on. "Your mom said your uncle was hiding plastic Easter eggs for their passengers to find."

Marge continued talking as I completely zoned out. Plastic Easter eggs. Seniors tripping and falling in the woods. Broken hips. Liability. Lawsuits galore. Full details on the 11PM news. I hate my life.

When I hung up, I calmly explained what Miss Hippity and Uncle Hoppity were up to. Ernie reminded me of the time Barbara, one of our former escorts who was now the Hartley franchise owner in East Providence, held a scavenger hunt with her passenger alongside the same parkway.

"That was totally different, Barbara's bus broke down and she did that to pass the time until a rescue bus arrived. When she got back I thanked her for her creativity but admonished her for putting her passengers in a clearly unsafe situation by letting them leave the safety of the coach."

The Kids eventually bunny hopped their way into Atlantic City hours behind schedule, once again missing their time slot for their first casino visit. As part of the tour, each passenger was to be given the casino's package of $15 in quarters and a dinner buffet worth $20. We were very fortunate we were able to reschedule their visit otherwise it would have cost us $3,500 to provide this casino package to each passenger on both buses.

When he left the office, Ernie did remind me, "One good thing, boss, at least they stayed on the route like you told them."

15. Shakespeare's At It Again

Miss Lynn's career in the travel industry was over, and don't think the entire travel community, especially me, wasn't grateful. Life went on. Mom hosted her card games, and I ran Hartley Tours.

For once in Mom's life, she was relatively calm and sane and, I thought, rooted in reality. She was nearing retirement age, maybe she was tired of the drama, but within months she was bored with "this whole retirement thing" and decided she wanted a job working with other retired people.

Within a month she was the newest AARP employment counselor in their Woonsocket, Rhode Island office. As she explained her position, she would be contacting area businesses and championing the cause of hiring seasoned, experienced older people. Maybe "championing the cause" isn't entirely accurate. Based on subsequent stories she told me, her favorite tactic was using the force of her personality to strong-arm employers into hiring *her* seniors.

This position was ideal for Mom. She was once again in control and doing what she did best, coercing businesses into buying her product (seniors) or else. The *or else* might include, oh I don't know, maybe an age discrimination charge or lawsuit. Miss Lynn became a saint, an Eva Peron, to the seniors seeking employment as she was always willing to help "the little people."

I really thought this was a win-win-win situation. A win for businesses being exposed to seniors, who would bring a lifetime of talent and experience to their companies. A win for older people over retirement age, now able to supplement their incomes with jobs previously unobtainable. A win for Mom, using her talent to unite the two and score one for "the little people."

It was not until I sifted through her papers after her death that I discovered all was not kosher. The resume she submitted for the job stated Mom graduated from Salve Regina College in Newport, RI. Although Mom had a wealth of street-smarts and could more than handle the position, her only formal education beyond high school was hairdressing school. Even so, I remember Mom talking about her time at Salve when I was a kid. Over the years, I think she came to believe it herself. Ironically my wife is the only family member having graduated from Salve Regina.

Occasionally on a Saturday while I was working, Mom would stop by to visit with Kathy and the kids. Realizing Kathy's full time teaching job left her little time to run errands during the week, Mom would insist that Kathy go out and do whatever she had to do and Mom would watch the children. This was a great gift on both sides. Kathy received some much needed help, and Mom was able to re-enter her grandchildren's lives as their nana.

(In a letter you will read shortly, contrary to our feeling that Mom enjoyed spending these Saturdays with her grandchildren, she claimed that she was being used as a babysitter because "you have no other" babysitters. As she stated in a subsequent letter, she wanted to be paid as a sitter just as Eleanor, our fulltime babysitter, was paid. So much for re-entering the grandchildren's lives as their nana.)

On one of these Saturdays, Kathy and I met for lunch like we used to BK (Before Kids) and wondered what kind of cookie lunch Mom was serving up the kids. I said, "No offense, Kathy, but later in their lives they'll probably forget all of your healthy meals while recalling their grandfather's cheese balls spoiling their dinners and Nana's cookie sandwich lunches."

During one of these Nana Saturdays, all of the kids from the houses on our circle were playing basketball while Mom sat on our front steps and watched. Mark, our youngest boy, ran over to her crying and told her the other kids said he was "DK." Mom not being up to speed in kid jargon asked him what "DK" meant. He responded, "Doesn't 'k'ount. They won't let me play with them."

Thems were fightin' words to my mother. "We'll show them. Get in the car. We're going to the store to buy you your own basketball hoop and pole. Then when they try and play with you, you tell them that they're DK."

And that's exactly what Mom and DK did. Of course, when I arrived home for dinner Mom pestered me more than Mark did to install the pole, which involved anchoring it into cement. Later that night I said to Kathy: "Not only do we have a kid that doesn't 'k'ount, he can't spell either."

Mom underwent hip replacement surgery. This type of surgery has become routine with over 300,000 hips replaced each year. Mom's surgery was equally routine and her complete recovery involved a short stay in the hospital's rehabilitation unit. Midway through her stay, she called telling me it was an emergency that I get to the rehab unit immediately. When I tried to probe the nature of the emergency, she said, "They're trying to kill me" and hung up.

I called the nurse's desk and told one of the nurses of my bizarre conversation with Mom. She said she would check on her and call me right back. "Your mom's fine. She's eating her breakfast."

When Kathy and I went to the facility to visit later that afternoon, Mom said we shouldn't talk in her room because it was bugged. "THEY could hear us."

She led us into the unoccupied physical therapy room and told me to close the doors. She then proceeded to tell us about the nurses who were in her room the night before, standing around her bed laughing and plotting how they were going to murder her.

I told her she must have had a nightmare, which she denied. Her bed-ridden roommate would have seen something. "Let's ask her about this."

"No. She's in on it. She was standing there with them; it's all an act that she can't walk and has to stay in bed. You've got to get me out of here before I'm dead."

While we walked her back to her room, I commented about how well her physical therapy was working: "You're a regular speed demon with that walker."

Mom claimed the physical therapists were useless and that she was the one who did her own physical therapy, which she could continue in the safety of her own apartment far away from the killer nurses.

Before we left, we spoke with Mom's nurse, who was delighted with her progress. I told her about Mom's fears that the nurses were conspiring to kill her and wondered whether her pain medication might be at the root of the problem. Her nurse responded that some patients on heavy-duty pain medications like morphine could experience hallucinatory moments, but she assured me this wasn't the case with Mom since she was on a low-dose of pain medication. She said she would relay Mom's concerns to her doctor and the nurse administrator in charge of the rehab unit.

Shortly after arriving home I received a call from Liz, Mom's longtime friend and pregnancy buddy. Liz said she'd just hung up the phone with Mom, who kept repeating "morte, morte, morte" (death, death, death) over and over. I told Liz about my morning call from Mom and our afternoon visit. I said the rehab staff was being made aware of Mom's mental state.

The following day when Kathy and I went to see Mom, there was a nurse sitting outside her door facing the room. Mom smiled and waved to the nurse and said, "This is my son and his wife."

She then motioned for us to move closer to her and said, "They put her out there to make sure I don't escape. They want to kill me right in this bed when the coast is clear. I know too much."

I looked out at the nurse, who continued reading a book. "What is it you know?"

Again Mom motioned us closer. "I can't tell you; they'll kill you too."

Once again we stopped at the nurse's station on our way out and were told the rehab administrator had ordered Mom to be placed under twenty-four hour surveillance. This was a precautionary measure. If she believed people were in her room attempting to murder her, she might try to get out of bed quickly, fall and injure herself.

Mom's rehab progress continued over the next four weeks while her allegations of nocturnal death squad visitors targeting her diminished. By the time she was discharged, she was the Mario Andretti of walkers. We brought her home and went grocery shopping to make sure she was well stocked. One of her neighbors offered to handle her future weekly food needs.

When our children were young, it was always a problem deciding how to split the holidays between Kathy's family, my dad's family and my mother. We finally rotated among all three for each holiday. It was always a problem when the holiday was at Mom's tiny studio apartment. Because of its size and the size of our family, we tried to get her to come to our house, but without success. And Mom's cooking, by her own admission, had not improved with age. Her specialty was emptying cans of Progresso soup into a large pot and then doctoring it up by tossing in hardboiled eggs still in their shells.

On the holidays we spent with Dad's family or Kathy's family, Mom would call to tell us one of my cousins had called and insisted she spend the holiday with his or her family because "no mother should be left alone on a holiday." To make sure we got the message, she would add, "Your cousin thinks it's awful the way you cast me aside like a rag to spend the holiday with *the other end"* (or the variation: Your cousin thinks it's awful the way you cast me aside like a rag to spend the holiday with your wife's family).

A few weeks before Thanksgiving when our children were very young, Mom called with the idea of all of us enjoying the Thanksgiving holiday on the Cape (Cape Cod, MA) with her. I had to decline because we had spent the previous Thanksgiving with her and this year we were scheduled to spend it with Dad's family. The following year, according to our schedule of being fair to all sides, we would be joining Kathy's family for Thanksgiving.

This did not sit well with Miss Lynn. She penned this:

Andy + Kathy

Since I never have any quality time with you two to discuss ANYTHING, I find a letter is my only means of communication. People would never believe my continued ugly relationship with you two. I am, as usual – just there when needed, to do whatever needed and to run for the children since you have no other. I remember very vividly when I was refused to care for Kristen for a day or hours however I'll move on –

Following our argument yesterday – I told you Kathy that I would not be available any longer – following this week. This "rag" is going to work full time and make a decent pay so I can "put food in my mouth." As I told you yesterday –

Monday was the last time, you called me up to join you for dinner with no strings attached. Strange – how everything is one sided in your house but when it comes to the bottom line – the "rag" is always available. As for Thanksgiving – "what do I have to be thankful for being in your company?" To sit with the children and talk as I always do when visiting. I love them – but once and a while it would have been great to have a few minutes to talk to MY ONLY SON. Since you two have been married, this has not been possible. You say you could not afford going to the Cape – have I ever made a suggestion and not covered all due tabs.

We would have taken the children there and returned to my place for turkey or I would have been happy to pay for all the meals at the Cape but I thought it would have been great for the kids to go see the Mayflower and how the pilgrims lived – (not necessary to go inside) then to my place, for a change for turkey. But as usual MRS. SIMMONS – the rag – will spend it as always –

Please be sure to work on a babysitter now as I will be employed full time as of next week.

If you wanted to save money – start at home then your many foolish parties and the numerous gifts you buy – you will find more money in your pocket.

The Rag

IF you save money at home – you would not have to work all the hours you do and would spend the very needed time with those precious children.

...

Christmas was a tricky holiday. In the Italian tradition it would involve two major get-togethers: Christmas Eve Dinner and Christmas Day Dinner. Whenever our holiday rotation involved our not being with Mom for either of those gatherings, we would take her out to lunch on Christmas Eve day and then return to her apartment to exchange gifts.

Christmas Day we would call Mom in the morning to wish her a Merry Christmas. She would be upbeat while talking to Kathy or me, but when each of the children took the phone she would deliver special holiday messages to them:

"This could be your nana's last Christmas before I die, I wanted to spend it seeing you but your mommy and daddy won't let me."

"Nana will be spending Christmas all by herself because your mommy and daddy want you to spend Christmas with your mommy's family."

Or the variation: "Nana will be spending Christmas all by herself because your mommy and daddy want you to spend Christmas with your Grandfather Big Andrew's family."

As the children grew older and wanted to spend all of the holidays at our house, Mom was invited to spend every holiday with us. Most holidays she would join us regardless of who was here from *the other end.*

On Christmas Day we would have Mom arrive earlier than everyone else to enjoy breakfast and open her gifts from us. We would go overboard buying gifts for Mom, because most years we were the only ones giving her Christmas presents. An added advantage to having Mom arriving early was that it gave her time alone with us and the grandkids before the rest of the guests arrived.

On Christmases when Dad's family was here, it was amazing how well she was able to get along with *the other end,* though Kathy and I would still hold our breath, anticipating a Miss Lynn detonation when we least expected it.

As our children grew even older, so did Nana. And so did her demands. In recent years, as soon as we were all sitting down for dinner, Mom would turn to me and say she was full from all of the pickings before the meal and wanted to be driven home. The first time she did this, I left everyone and drove her home, which took an hour to get there and back. After 30 minutes or so listening to her complain about *the other end,* and how badly we treated her, by the time I got back home every bit of Christmas cheer had been sucked out of me.

At the next holiday gathering, she did the very same thing: Sat down to dinner and demanded I take her home. Kristen and Michael, our middle son, got to their feet and volunteered to drive Nana home, but Mom insisted that they stay put. She didn't want to interrupt their dinner. She wanted me to drive her for obvious reasons. Here was another opportunity to lash out at me about the way Kathy and I treated her like "Second Hand Rose," the "rag."

"No, Nana. Dad is staying here. We're taking you home."

I pity Mom on that drive. Both Kristen and Michael are brutally honest and quite capable of seeing right through Mom's delusions and lies.

These are the same two of our children who picked up Mom to drive her to the hospital to see me after my heart bypass surgery while I was still in the ICU. They cautioned her and repeated what they'd been told by one of the ICU nurses. Don't react to anything you see. Where there was extensive stapling from all of the veins removed, there might be bleeding. There might be bleeding around the tubes inserted in my body. At first my mother objected to them telling her what to do, and said I was her son, and she would respond any way she damn well pleased. Michael said, "In that case you're not going into the ICU."

She eventually promised to control herself and broke that promise as soon as she walked into the ICU. I was told later that the drive back to her apartment was rather unpleasant, with Mom her usual complaining, irrational self, and the kids calling her on everything she said. That ride didn't end well for Mom. *Something told me this one wouldn't, either.*

When Mom tried to complain about Kathy and me, the kids told her they were amazed their mother still spoke to her. "The fact that our mom still calls you "Mom" after the way you've treated her is more than we could do. And that Dad keeps bothering with you after the way you've treated him is more than we could ever do."

According to Kristen and Michael, from that point on there was total silence from the back seat until they arrived back at Mom's place. After she got out of the car, she turned and delivered a last, parting jab: "Someday both of you will know the truth about your parents.

Kathy and I, both products of Catholic school guilt, felt sorry for Mom, regardless. After Kristen and Michael told us about the drive home, I called Mom, intending to have a pleasant conversation with her about how she might spend the rest of the day. Mom said that she didn't want me – or anyone else from our family, including the children – to call her ever again unless we could speak to her with the respect she deserved.

"If respect means you expect our children to sit and listen to you bad mouth their parents, it's not going to happen."

"Of course it's not. You and your wife have brainwashed your children against me."

"No, you've done that all by yourself." The next sound was of the phone slamming.

I turned to Kathy, gave her the gist, and added that we should probably stand by the mailbox, because no doubt, "Shakespeare is at it again even as we speak."

The letters started arriving a couple of days later, along with a series of voice mail messages left on my cell phone telling me never to call her again. Ever. "My son is dead to me BUT when you do return my call, Andrew, my name is Ms. Simmons to you."

Don't ever call me again, and when you do, call me Ms. Simmons. That makes perfect sense.

Included in the voice mail messages was a "subtle" (Miss Lynn is never subtle) threat to tell my children about my first marriage. When I was 19, I married a young woman, who turned out to have severe psychological problems dating back to childhood. During our brief nine month marriage she spent time in the psychiatric unit of a local hospital and eventually went to live with her mom, who lived out of state.

The marriage was annulled, and Mom got herself a lot of leverage, or thought she had. All these years this Sword of Damocles had been dangling over my head. At least to Mom's way of thinking. She pulled it out and threatened to tell the kids from time to time, and my response was always go and do whatever you have to do.

I could let this roll off my back, while gentle, sensitive Kathy could not. Over the past 35 years, Mom took absolute pleasure in calling Kathy by the name of my first "wife". Kathy would never respond, of course, but her eyes showed her hurt.

Life took on a weird normalcy after that, a rhythm of nasty phone calls, poison pen letters, and changing plans about where she was going to leave her wealth. She had blown through all of the GANBC money. The money from the sale of The Big House was also gone. All of her savings accounts were running on empty. This left her living on her monthly Social Security check, plus any revenue from her occasional poker parties, clandestinely held in the large mail room of her senior citizen apartment complex.

When I pointed out her financial condition, she told me I didn't know what I was talking about. Insisted she had millions of dollars stashed away from her PowerBall Lottery and Publishers Clearing House winnings. Don't we all?

This jogged a memory of Mom calling one day to tell me she received a Publishers Clearing House letter: "It was even addressed to ME." She was expecting a call soon telling her she had won the PCH jackpot. I told her it was only a direct mail ploy mass mailed to millions of others to get her to subscribe to their magazines. She hadn't actually won anything.

She became indignant and yelled into the phone, "Ever since you were young, you always dragged me down. This time you're not, junior. And you're not getting any of my money."

Mom was getting worse. Later when we cleaned out her apartment, the only communication from Publisher's Clearing House were stacks of magazines – most not even out of their plastic mail wraps - strewn about her apartment.

During this time period I was battling another diabetes complication. This would give me the diabetic trifecta: Heart problems, vision impairment, and now kidney failure. When I told Mom I was going to need a kidney transplant, she offered to be tested to see if she was a match and give me one of hers. I jokingly said, "No way. If they test you, they'll want to yank whatever organs are still functioning in me and transplant them into you." She was one of the few that offered to be a living donor for me, and that was a touching offer.

In June of 2012 I received a late night call from Florida Hospital. They had a kidney match. As I packed for Orlando, Florida, I called Mom to let her know what was going on and promised her Kathy would be in constant communication to keep her updated.

The surgery went perfectly. Unfortunately, I had heart related issues which caused an elevated blood pressure. After a week in the multi-service ICU, I was moved to the regular transplant floor. In a matter of hours, my blood pressure soared to 200+ over 110. I was rushed first to the cardiac ICU and then returned to the multi-service ICU. While doctors and nurses filled my room to work on me, another nurse walked in holding a phone. Handing it to me she said, "Your mother wants to speak to you."

Woozy from the medication and only vaguely conscious of what was going on all around me, I put the phone to my ear and heard Mom bellowing, "What's the matter with Kathy? I just called her and she's not answering when she sees it's my number on her phone." I handed the phone back to the nurse.

I had stabilized by early evening and was conscious enough to ask Kathy if she was in touch with Mom. Kathy said she updated Mom each morning and each evening. I told her about my mother's call. Kathy explained she was in the middle of a conversation with Mom when she saw me being rushed from the transplant floor to the cardiac ICU, and she quickly told Mom she'd call her back as soon as she knew anything. Kathy had called Mom when she received word that I was stable.

When our son, Michael, who was at the hospital with Kathy, heard about Mom's latest call, he went to the ICU's desk and put a password protection on any incoming calls to me while I was in the ICU. He was immediately asked about my mother, who was constantly calling them. Michael told them he didn't want me bothered by phone calls, especially the ones from her.

Our daughter, Kristen, became engaged while I was recuperating in Florida. When we told Mom, her first response was, "She'd better have her wedding up here in Rhode Island rather than Baltimore. I went to plenty of weddings and gave a lot of money. It's time they reciprocated. Besides she's my granddaughter, I should have some say where she gets married." I told her it was strictly up to Kristen where she wanted to have her wedding. She chose Baltimore.

Save-the-date cards were sent out for their August wedding. Mom and her friend Liz, who was going to accompany Mom, each received one. Not too long after, Kathy and I sent out invitations to come to an engagement party we would host in December when Kristen and Jamison, her fiancé, would be up from Baltimore for Christmas.

Both Mom and Liz received engagement party invitations. Mom called to ask why Jeanne, Liz's daughter and my friend from birth, was not included. I told her that I had already discussed this with Kristen. Because Jeanne could not be invited to the wedding due to guest limits imposed on both sets of parents, it would be improper to invite Jeanne and her husband, Frank, to the engagement party. Mom called me every night for weeks trying to get me to talk to Kristen about reconsidering. Kristen always said no. Our last conversation about the engagement party ended with an ultimatum. "If Jeanne isn't invited, Liz will not go. If Liz does not go, I will not go." All this drama over an engagement party and not getting her own way.

We once again invited Mom to spend Christmas Day with the family, including our new addition, Kristen's Jamison. Mom said her legs were bothering her, and she didn't want to be away from home all day. Instead, she wanted to go out to lunch Christmas Eve day. Even though we had plans for last minute food and gift shopping, we decided to work around them to accommodate Mom.

A few weeks prior to Christmas I sent a group email to the kids asking for a family meeting sometime while they were all home. This triggered a texting frenzy between the four of them as they wondered what it was all about. Matthew, our oldest son, came to me and said, "What's the big deal, it's because you're downsizing and selling the house, right?" I played along and asked him how he found out about the pending sale.

When we gathered for our meeting, I looked around our family room. Kristen and Jamison were living together, no problem telling them. Ditto for Matthew, who was living with Katie, a lovely girl. And I didn't think it would be all that earth shattering to either Michael or Mark.

"In 1970 when I was 19, there was no such thing as living with someone prior to marriage. I met a girl, thought it was love, and married her. Our marriage lasted nine months. She had psychological problems dating back to her youth. During our marriage she was under continuous psychiatric care. She also spent a good deal of time trying to straighten out her life back at her mom's place in Maine. Our marriage was annulled."

Silence.

Michael was the first to speak, "That's it? That's what you wanted to tell us? Who cares?"

Oh, yeah, that sword is *gone.*

16. The Final Turn

Mid-May Mom called to tell me she was experiencing a great deal of pain in her legs and feet. I asked if she had called her doctor, she said, "What's that going to do. He won't call me back. And even if he does, I'm not going to agree with what he says."

I told her I was going to call for a rescue squad; she said each senior apartment had a call button which would get faster service. She pressed it and said she had to pack a few things and hung up.

When we arrived at the hospital, Mom was in the emergency room while doctors were attempting to determine the cause of her acute leg and foot pain. More tests yielded inconclusive results. Therefore it was determined the best course of action would be to admit her for observation and further testing. Although she resisted and wanted to go home, I told her leaving the hospital was not possible.

Since blood was detected in her stool, a gastroenterologist was called in for a consult. He determined a colonoscopy was in order and scheduled the procedure. When we walked into Mom's room the next day, the sheet was tented over her feet and lower legs due to the pain she was experiencing when the sheet touched her body.

Two days later the colonoscopy was performed. The doctor called with the results: There was a growth that might be cancerous, but he could not be certain until the tissue sample he removed was scrutinized by the lab. With my limited knowledge of colon cancer, I asked him if it had pierced the wall of her intestines. He said it had and that he would get back to me as soon as he heard from the lab.

Visiting Mom later that day we found her groggy from the procedure and in good spirits. As a matter of fact, she saw no reason to linger in the hospital and wanted to return to her apartment. That was out of the question, of course, since we hadn't heard from the lab. Of even more concern was her inability to stand or walk without experiencing severe pain.

The gastroenterologist called me once the lab results were in: They couldn't be sure if it was cancer or not. This is 2013 not 1913, people. With today's technology you cannot determine if cells are cancerous or not?

His recommended course of action was to release Mom to a rehab center. This would allow her time to heal from the colonoscopy, and would also include physical therapy to hopefully make her more mobile. He would then repeat the procedure in four weeks.

The hospital called as soon as we'd hung up and asked me if I had a rehab facility preference. I told her this was a first and I had no idea. My only experience was when Mom was at the hospital's own rehab unit. The person said their rehab unit would not be possible. No kidding. Not after what Mom put them through the last time recuperating from her hip replacement surgery. She said she would call around to area treatment centers to see where there was availability and call me back. Later in the day Mom was transported to a rehab facility and nursing home. I was relieved to learn they catered to elderly care.

During this period, I was recuperating from my kidney transplant. With my immune system compromised, I was warned to wear a surgical mask when visiting Mom.

Although Mom's two bedded room was small, it didn't seem to bother her. The repetitive questions Mom asked every few minutes concerned me, as it was consistent with a fairly advanced stage of dementia.

"Why am I here? Why can't I go home? Who put me in here?" We would explain she was there to receive physical therapy in order to be able to walk and move around on her own again. A couple of minutes later: "Why am I here? Why can't I go home? Who put me in here?"

"I'm dying, you know." We assured her this was not the case according to her doctor. I attempted a little humor, "You've been dying for as long as I can remember." Waving her finger in the air, "This time I'm really going." I laughed, "Really? Going where? Atlantic City? Maybe we'll join you on your trip." She laughed too.

Mom spoke of needing clothes from her apartment, so we took her keys and drove to Lincoln Manor. Walking into Mom's apartment was like walking into a dumpster. The putrid odor was nauseating. Thank God, I had brought my hospital mask with me.

While I quickly opened the windows, Kathy dashed to Mom's bureau drawers and closet to seek the requested clothing items. "Andrew, everything's dirty. We can't bring Mom any of these." I agreed with Kathy, lowered the windows to allow at least a crack of fresh air to flow into the apartment and we left as rapidly as we entered.

On the way back to the rehab center, we stopped at a mall to purchase new outfits and underclothing for Mom. Kathy drove me insane with the fastidious manner in which she selected every item. I married a saint. With all of the pain and heartache my mother caused Kathy over the years, how could she possibly be so finicky, carefully picking out the clothes she thought would look best on Mom?

As Kathy showed Mom each blouse, pair of slacks and sweater prior to hanging them in Mom's closet, I can honestly say Mom was excited and grateful for all of the new clothing. She did ask why we didn't bring her her own instead of spending our money on new clothes. Not having the heart to tell her they were filthy, Kathy fibbed and said it was easier to go to the mall rather than drive all the way to her place in Lincoln.

1:35AM. Our phone startles us out of sleep.

"I have to go to the bathroom." I told Mom to ring the nurse's call button on the side of her bed. "Don't you think I know that? She's not coming on purpose. I want you to come here and bring me a bedpan now."

I explained we lived over a half-hour away and it would be easier for her to ring the nurse's call button again. Click. A few minutes pass, our phone rings again, "I know they're trying to kill me by not letting me go to the bathroom. And you're in on it too.

Calmly I told Mom no one was trying to kill her and that I would call the nurse for her. When I spoke to the nurse, she told me Mom had been sitting on a bedpan – for the third time - for the past twenty minutes. The first and second times had been false alarms.

A few weeks passed with Mom receiving daily physical therapy and, more importantly, nourishing meals. During one of our visits, we were chatting when all of a sudden Mom's face contorted and took on a look of horror. She asked me who was in back of her bed. I told her the only thing in back of the bed was a wall. "You're lying. There's someone there." Again I told her that no one was there. "Yes, there is. He's trying to kill me." I assured her no one was trying to kill her. Raising her finger in my face she said someone was trying to kill her and she was going to get to the bottom of it. She intended to find out the real reason she was there and what kind of medicine they were giving her so she could not walk.

On our way out, we met with her nurse and I told her what had just happened. I requested that she be seen by a neurologist as soon as possible.

A few days later, my cousin Johnny (on my father's side, you know, *the other end*) picked me up and drove me to the rehab facility for a meeting to discuss Mom's progress and recommendations for her future care. Prior to the meeting, I met with her caseworker, who asked me questions about my mother's mental state. I spoke of Mom's spates of confusion, repetitiveness and how she was convinced someone was behind her bed planning to kill her. I also recounted Mom's family history of dementia: One brother who died as a result of Alzheimer's, another brother and a sister who were in advanced stages of Alzheimer's, and another younger sister who was in the early stages.

The rest of the team arrived for the meeting. Mom was brought there in a wheelchair. Upon entering she greeted my cousin Johnny, aware that she had not seen him in many years. She also acknowledged the presence of various members of the team, greeting them cordially. Not a word was said to me, it was as though I wasn't even there.

When asked why she was there, Mom said she was there because certain people wanted her there, out of their way. She added she felt fine and perfectly able to care for herself at home. Her caseworker reminded her of her inability to walk, which would be an obstacle to her returning home without assistance in her day to day activities.

In terms of her mobility, it was determined that initially Mom was making very little progress in rehabilitating herself. However over the past week or so, there was a noticeable change for the better as Mom exhibited signs of exerting herself during the physical therapy sessions. Therefore, they concluded in compliance with Medicare regulations she could remain in rehab status for a few more weeks before being reevaluated.

After Mom was wheeled from the room, the caseworker who had observed the way Mom ignored me, asked if I thought Mom recognized me. I replied that I was sure she did, but intentionally would not acknowledge me because she considered me one of "those people" who put her there to keep her out of the way.

I thought the meeting went well. Johnny and I accompanied Mom up to her floor and sat with her during a cognitive therapy session. Occasionally she would turn and ask Johnny a question about the old neighborhood, the neighborhood where members of Dad's family lived, where Johnny still resides. Amazingly her recall was spot on, not all that unusual for those having dementia as their long term memory is at times quite good.

Before leaving, the final person I had to meet with was the facility's business manager who was charged with gathering financial information about how the patient's care was going to be paid for once she had used up the allotted Medicare covered days. Although I was uncertain of Mom's finances, I told her based on how Mom was living, it was doubtful she had any savings remaining. She offered to assist me in filing for Medicaid coverage for the anticipated $8,000+ monthly patient care and maintenance fee.

That weekend Kathy and I searched Mom's apartment for any financial information to help us complete the Medicaid application form. We searched for bank statements, insurance policies, savings account books and a safety deposit key. The only record we found was a single page from a three month old bank statement; it was found behind her desk probably having fallen from the top of the desk.

Analyzing her statement, the only source of income was a direct deposit monthly social security check. After she paid her modest monthly living expenses she would be left with one thousand dollars.

There were frequent ATM withdrawals at Lincoln's Twin Rivers Casino, a few miles from Mom's residence, and a social club in nearby Woonsocket. The amount of cash withdrawn on that statement was around one thousand dollars.

I would have to account for these cash transactions in the event I was questioned as a result of the Medicaid filing. Usually the state will probe cash transactions over the previous five years. All cash should have been exhausted paying for the patient's care prior to Medicaid assuming the financial burden. If not, where did the cash go? To whom did the cash go?

When I questioned Mom about the ATM withdrawals, she claimed she had no idea. I asked her how frequently she went to Twin Rivers Casino over the twelve years since the casino opened and she emphatically stated she had only been there once, possibly twice. I asked her again if she was sure she had not been there on a weekly basis over the past year and she reiterated her claim of having been there only twice over the twelve years since it opened. Then I moved on to the social club in Woonsocket and the cash withdrawals made there. She said she had never been to any social club in Woonsocket.

With so many ATM withdrawals, I asked her how she didn't notice them listed on her monthly bank statements. She said she threw her bank statements away without opening them. To get her bank balance she said it was easier calling the bank's automated account information line. (Consistent with the way in which Mom conducted her business going back to the GANBC Canary Islands days.)

I asked her where her ATM card was, and she said she had it with her in her wallet which was in her handbag. Checking her wallet, I discovered the ATM card was missing.

If she was a regular at the casino, she should have had a Twin Rivers Rewards card for the freebies which no senior citizen would let slip through his/her fingers. No Rewards card. When I asked her about it, she responded why would she even have one since she only was there once or twice.

We moved on to the next item I needed for the Medicaid filing: Life insurance. "Oh, yes, I have plenty of policies. They're in the large envelope I gave to you a couple of years ago." Then it dawned on me, she had in fact given me a manila envelope when Matthew drove me to visit with her, and it had "do not open until my death" written on the outside.

When we returned home, I opened the manila envelope and found a number of insurance policy offers to the effect of 'if you purchase so much of our insurance, we will also include a free $1,000 insurance policy absolutely free." Of course Mom, like most seniors, will see the huge headline of "$1,000 of life insurance absolutely free" and think they were covered. She had no life insurance coverage to list on the Medicaid application.

Mom's bank was next on my agenda. Since I was on her account, I would be able to obtain copies of Mom's bank statements over the past year to further add to her Medicaid application. I glanced at the only bank statement we found and saw Mom's name and my cousin Carol and her husband's names on the account. My name had been removed from Mom's account.

The only thing upsetting to me about having been removed from her account was that I wouldn't be able to immediately secure the documents I needed. Plus, I would have to ask my cousin to go to the bank and get them for me, thereby inconveniencing her and causing a delay in the Medicaid filing. A few days later Carol called to let me know she had the year's worth of bank statements.

Consistent with the single statement we found, casino and social club ATM withdrawals over the previous year totaled just shy of ten thousand dollars. I pumped the numbers into an Excel spreadsheet hoping to find a pattern. The social club withdrawals would occur on the same day each week whereas the casino withdrawals would occur on various days.

Kathy and I returned to Mom's apartment prior to visiting her as I wanted to pick-up her answering machine, which had the maximum of 25 recorded messages the last time we were there. Perhaps one of those messages would be from a caller who would drive her to the casino or social club since she had not driven in years.

When we walked in, we noticed two plastic cards on the floor alongside her desk and one on the edge of her desk. The plastic cards on the floor: an ATM card and a SNAP card (food assistance for the elderly). The plastic card on the desk's edge: Twin River's Rewards card.

This was an unexpected sight since we had previously cleared Mom's desk off completely. And the likelihood of the two of us walking over the white plastic cards on top of a dark green carpet was impossible.

One thing bothered me beyond our stumbling on the cards we were seeking: Was there a duplicate key to Mom's apartment? And if so, who had it? Someone had obviously been here to leave the cards. And, since Mom claimed to only have been to the casino "once, possibly twice since it opened", whoever had the key could have been using Mom's ATM card.

Questioning Mom about a duplicate key to her place was met with flat out denial. She had had the same key for the eighteen years she had lived at Lincoln Manor and never had a copy made. When I showed her the itemized ATM withdrawals, she said it was a fake document, and she wanted the person's name and telephone number who made it to prove they were lying. I said I compiled the information from her bank statements and handed them to her. After looking at them she said maybe someone was using her ATM card without her knowledge.

This might have been true. Mom had told me a while back that she was unable to walk beyond her apartment down the corridor to retrieve her mail. How could she walk through a casino or to a social club? As far as I knew, outside of doctor appointments, the last time she walked out of her apartment was when we brought her to lunch Christmas Eve day to meet our daughter's fiancé. After that she wanted to remain in her apartment, in her favorite chair during our visits with her cane by her side. Yet her ATM withdrawals continued throughout the winter right through mid-May until she was hospitalized.

On our way home, I told Kathy Mom's ATM case was worthy of the CSI series. She promptly dubbed me CSI: Andy.

The following day I emailed the administrator of Lincoln Manor to brief her on what I had uncovered and to make her aware that other residents may have fallen victim to or will fall victim to being ATM scammed. I also asked Lincoln Manor's management if Mom ever had copies of her apartment key made.

I received an email from the property manager stating that the previous September, Mom called their office and said she had lost her apartment key and would need a duplicate. They provided her with their master key for her apartment and instructed her to have the local locksmith make copies for her and then return the original to the office.

My cousin Zee, Carol's husband, who lived nearby, confirmed that he drove her to the locksmith and the key was copied. The Manor's master key was returned to them. That same day, someone found Mom's lost keys, including her apartment key, in the parking lot in front of her apartment building and turned them in to the office. They were returned to Mom.

So contrary to Mom's statement, there was another key to her apartment. And someone had definitely left her cards after Kathy and I had already searched for them.

With this information I called the RI Department of Elderly Affairs to report the possibility that someone was preying on a senior citizen. They said they would pursue it and encouraged me to contact an officer on the Lincoln Police Department who handled cases involving senior citizens.

An officer at the Lincoln Police Department took my report. I gave him photocopies of the bank statements as well as Mom's ATM and Twin Rivers' Rewards cards. I told him that they would probably have a better shot of finding the person who withdrew the money by looking at the social club's ATM machine's digital photo file to see who was using the ATM card. It would be more difficult to find it at one of the casino's ATMs with so many transactions from so many machines. I also provided him with a list of the only people I knew from Lincoln Manor who knew Mom, along with a list of those who called and left a message on her answering machine while she was hospitalized, quite a few wondering where Mom was since she was not at the club (which I assumed it was others who frequented the Woonsocket social club).

I left the police station pretty sure they viewed everyone as a suspect in these types of cases. Even CSI: Andy.

The next day my cousin Zee called me. He was disturbed over a phone call from the Lincoln PD. I explained what the investigation was all about. He said the person I should speak to about my mother's visits to the casino was my Aunt Joan.

Auntie Joan was married to my mother's brother Al who had passed away. She was always one of my favorites, brazenly telling you the truth whether you wanted to hear it or not. I called her and told her what Mom said about going to Twin Rivers Casino once or twice since it opened.

"Are you kidding, Andy? She's not telling you the truth. She went to the casino once or twice a week." Her statement was consistent with the ATM withdrawals. Auntie added when she was not at the casino she would go to some club in Woonsocket to play cards. This provided even more consistency to the pattern of ATM withdrawals.

In order that the Lincoln Police Department not waste any more time on the case, I notified them of my conversation with Auntie Joan. I also contacted Lincoln Manor to allay any fear that someone was taking advantage of their residents.

To this day, before I roll the credits and close out this episode of CSI: Andy, three things still bother me:

ONE: How did the ATM, SNAP and Twin Rivers Casino Rewards cards mysteriously reappear?

TWO: Since we thoroughly cleaned out Mom's apartment and did not find any duplicate key, was it lost? Or does someone still have it?

THREE: Suffering with severe pain in her lower legs and feet, requiring a tent to keep the sheet off her body, how could Mom have walked to and from a casino or to and from a social club right up until a few days before her hospitalization?

One of Mom's out-of-state friends called me after speaking with Mom and asked me why she was being kept at the nursing facility against her wishes. I explained her mental and physical conditions and her inability to care for herself were keeping her from returning to independent living. She warned me that she would be visiting Mom before too long and, "God help you if what you're telling me isn't true." When I told Kathy of this conversation I added, "Birds of a feather…

During our next visit, Mom directed her conversation to me as though Kathy was not even in the room. At one point she did turn to Kathy and ordered her to, "Go and get me ginger ale."

Once Kathy was out of the room, she asked me "Is your house still in her name?" As I explained several other times when Mom asked me this same question, for business purposes it was placed under Kathy's name years ago.

"Put the house in your name, I don't trust her." Don't trust her? The same person who stood by my side throughout your relentless verbal and written abuse? The same woman who camped out and slept on a metal chair in my ICU room for 11 nights following my transplant, because I told her I didn't want to die alone? This is the woman you don't trust?

Kathy came back with Mom's ginger ale and held it for her so her distrusting mother-in-law could slowly take sips. When Mom was through, Kathy came over to me and whispered, "Andrew, you've got to get out of this room now."

After we left the room, Kathy told me to turn around and look at the floor around Mom's roommate's bed. It was puddled with urine. Passing the nurse's station, Kathy mentioned what we had seen and how this concerned her given Mom's still unknown underlying condition and my suppressed immune system.

In light of the kidney transplant, the next day I called one of my local medical offices for future visitation advice. I was told as long as I did not come in direct contact with the urine I would be fine. In response to this I did say that I always wear a mask when visiting the rehab/nursing facility. She questioned me as to why I was wearing a mask. "You can't live in a cocoon. It's nearly a year after your transplant. You don't wear a surgical mask to the supermarket do you?" I was taken aback by this statement and responded, "You're right I don't wear a mask when we go grocery shopping, but then again no one's pissing in the supermarket aisles."

Our next visit to Mom found her in a much larger room directly across the hall from her previous room (and incontinent roommate). It overlooked a high school's baseball field. Baseball had become a passion for Mom over the past decade. She could spout off stats and baseball trivia to rival any sportscaster covering the sport.

The gerontologist contacted me after meeting with Mom on three separate occasions. He found that Mom was having issues with dementia. However his next question nearly floored me. "How long has your mother been delusional?"

It was my turn to floor him. "Let me see, doctor. I'm 62 so I'd say for the past 62 years. Probably longer, before I was born."

Finally, FINALLY, someone else, an expert, put a tag on what I – not to mention many others - had lived with my entire life; a mother who resided and functioned in her own world, Miss Lynn's World, at times completely detached from reality.

The gerontologist further explained that since Mom identified Kathy as being "Out to get me right from the day she married my son," it would be best if Kathy didn't come with me to visit Mom. I told him this was not going to happen for two reasons: One, Kathy was the one responsible for our family's continued involvement in

Mom's life, because had it been up to me there would be as much distance between Mom and me as was humanly possible; and, two, with my vision impairment, Kathy was my means of transportation, and I sure as hell was not about to let her sit in the car or a waiting room while I visited.

During a visit with her longtime friend, Liz, Mom spoke of her desire to move to Charlesgate Nursing Facility, where Liz had been the Admissions Coordinator for over 30 years before she retired. As soon as Liz got home, she called me about Mom wanting to transfer. Liz said she would be willing to contact Charlesgate's administrator on our behalf and have me tour the facility before I made a decision.

On the Charlesgate tour, I was struck by the cleanliness and brightness of the halls, resident rooms and dining/community rooms on each floor. There were many patient activities going on. During my many visits to Mom's current rehab/nursing center, the only entertaining event I witnessed was a female patient who would frequently emerge from her room, walk to the nurse's station, and yell at them before serenely turning and walking back to her room.

From what I observed the Charlesgate staff and patients seemed friendly and, for the most part, happy. I was convinced Mom would be in her glory there.

Mom was excited about the move to Charlesgate when I told her. However getting her to understand when the move would be taking place proved problematic as she could not grasp the actual day of her move. The arrangements were made to transfer her on Thursday, three days away. She kept insisting that she had to pack her things as she would be moving to Charlesgate the next day. We would explain it was not tomorrow, not the next day but the day after. But she was unable to grasp the passage of days.

I assured her she would not have to pack anything as the nursing staff would handle that for her.

When my cousin Carol and her husband Zee stopped by for a visit, Mom enthusiastically informed them of her move. We all chatted for a while, and then Zee turned to my wife and said he had no idea she was so nice. God only knows what Mom said about Kathy and me to them (or the rest of her family) over the years.

Thursday came and Mom was transported to Charlesgate. Kathy and I were transported to Orlando, Florida for my first annual kidney transplant checkup at Florida Hospital/Orlando. My evaluation began early Friday morning and by noon there were three messages on my cell phone from my mother demanding to be returned to the previous facility as she hated Charlesgate. As if I was not already running a high blood pressure that day, I certainly did not need this.

I contacted the nurse in charge on Mom's floor who was aware of Mom's calls to me. I explained I was out-of-state at Florida Hospital and unable to come to Charlesgate to appease Mom. Speaking with her was soothing as she assured me it was only an adjustment problem. It appeared that Lynn was used to snapping her fingers and having people wait on her, whereas on the floor she was assigned to, patients were encouraged to stay active and do as much as they could for themselves. She continued, "You worry about yourself down there, your mom is well taken care of here."

Before returning to the hospital, I called Mom's friend Liz, who also told me Mom was going through a period of adjustment which was a common experience shared by most new Charlesgate patients. She said when we arrived back home from Florida on Monday, Mom would be well on her way to adapting to Charlesgate.

Perhaps Liz's timeline for Mom's adaptation to Charlesgate was a trifle optimistic. While visiting Monday night, Mom ordered me to move her back to the other rehab facility. I told her it was not possible as they no longer had an available bed for her, even though I knew they did. This triggered a major mood swing as cantankerous Lynn suddenly appeared once again yammering about this being a plot to kill her and adding a new twist: "Liz is in on it too, that's why she wanted me to come here."

"Really," I said. "And who told you that?"

She responded, "Wouldn't you like to know? My sources tell me everything, junior. Don't YOU forget that."

Taking the elevator down from Mom's floor, I looked at an exhausted Kathy. We had been in motion since 5AM, leaving Orlando for our return flight to Providence. "Welcome home," I said.

The doctor who performed Mom's second colonoscopy reported all went well and he was able to remove 85% of the growth. In 4 to 6 weeks he would do another colonoscopy to remove the remaining 15%. His response to my "Is it cancer or not?" was that he could not be sure.

Mom's spirits seemed to improve over the following weeks, or to put it another way, she was not overtly trying to buck the system quite as much. She was now participating in all of the activities, spending less time in her room and more time being a part of the patient community. Interacting with others in their common community/dining room did her a world of good.

A constant recurring question: "When can I go home?"

I was honest and told her probably never, because she was unable to live on her own anymore.

"I'm perfectly fine to go back to my place."

I told her she would never get strong based on what I found in her refrigerator. Her forgetfulness would also be a problem. "I found seven half-empty soda cans scattered around your one room apartment."

"No you didn't, you're a liar. I don't even drink soda. Someone else put them there, maybe you and Kathy."

Regardless, I told her she required assistance in mobility, having meals prepared for her and taking her medication as scheduled. Pointing to the building next door to the nursing center I said if she was once again able to walk and ate all of her healthy meals, she could probably live in the Charlesgate assistant living facility alongside the nursing/rehab building. There you would have your own apartment yet have all of your meals served to you in the dining room and have your medication dispensed by their nursing staff.

She would eat her meals at the corner table by the windows in order to look at the adjacent assisted living building. I'm sure she was relishing the thought of regaining more of her independence by moving there. Sitting at that particular table also came with another benefit: A man named Oscar. Leave it to Mom to find a new companion among the male nursing home population.

Oscar would rarely speak unless ordered to do so by Mom. Even on those occasions it would only be a nod, a smile, or a yes/no answer to her question. We never saw anyone visiting Oscar so we included him in our conversations, even though he simply sat there staring and listening.

While visiting one day, as we entered the community room we saw Oscar and Lynn at *their* special table with their window on the world; for Mom it was her window to semi-independent living. While chatting Mom turned to Kathy and me, put her hand over her mouth and whispered that Oscar was a "Multi, multi, multi, multi – did I say that four times? – millionaire." Leave it to Mom to find a man with a hefty balance sheet. Eat your heart out, David.

Facing a mid-July deadline we had to focus our attention on clearing out Mom's apartment. Just the thought of going back into that foul environment gave me palpitations. We came armed with every disinfecting cleaning product known to man, heavy duty rubber gloves, industrial masks, disinfectants, etc. We literally ran into Mom's apartment, opened the windows as wide as we could, opened six or seven room deodorizers, lavishly sprinkled the carpets with fragrant cleaning powder and ran out as fast as we ran in.

Giving the apartment time to absorb the new scents, we went on a shopping spree seeking more clothing for Mom and the rubber soled sneakers she needed for physical therapy.

A couple of hours later, we returned to the apartment and were pleasantly surprised at the magic that had taken place courtesy of the air and carpet fresheners. Kathy took charge of packing all of Mom's clothes; I concentrated on emptying the kitchen.

As soon as one of the senior citizen residents observed me making a trip to the dumpster with old pans and dishes, she stopped me from tossing them into the trash as she removed a pan of special interest to her. When questioned, I explained we were clearing everything out of my mother's apartment.

Forget social media, texting or tweeting, there's no faster communication than between senior citizens, especially if it involves free stuff. When I returned to take another load to the dumpster, other residents began flowing into the apartment to see which treasuries would fit nicely into their already cluttered apartments. In less than a half-hour, with the exception of Mom's mementos and clothing which we retained for her, practically everything was gone.

We then drove to the nursing center to bring Mom the additional clothing and sneakers we purchased for her. In trying on the three pairs of sneakers, none fit because her feet were swollen. Mom looked at Kathy's flip-flops and commented, "I bet those would fit me." A nurse recommended special "edema shoes" which we were able to order online.

Some visits Mom was alert and rational, others she was foggy and somewhat difficult. Once her much younger roommate spoke of Mom being a real cutup at the previous night's bingo game and having everyone in stitches. I looked at Mom while Wanda relayed this anecdote, and Mom's reaction was to mouth, "She's crazy," while her index finger did circles around her ear much like we did back in elementary school.

On our next visit Mom had turned completely against Wanda. Wanda was a drug dealing prostitute (hm, kind of like "wonderful person"?) and the police had come during the night to arrest her. But with Wanda's criminal connections she was able to avoid going to jail and doing any time. We asked one of the nurses at the nurses' station if Mom's story was fact or fiction. It was fiction, the nurse responded as no incident report was filed.

In yet another visit Mom had her personal fortune pegged at $390 million. (Good to hear since her checkbook balance was $370. Not 370 million, 370 dollars.) I asked her how she came up with that number and she said it was from an insurance settlement over an accident she had and David, her lawyer, was keeping track of all her funds. She added "I already told David about you and how you're not good with money at all, you don't care if you have twenty cents in your pocket or a million." It was in her will that David would only give me one million dollars a year. Only a mil a year? How's a guy gonna live on a mere million each year?

Kathy cleared her throat and nodded to look at the television screen. It was a commercial for PowerBall. The jackpot? $390 million. Mom must have seen that commercial a number of times – as did all the rest of us – and somehow the $390 million stuck in her head as belonging to her.

The third colonoscopy was performed and I was told the estimated remaining 15% of the tumor was fully removed. How can *it* – for argument sake let's call *it* what it is: cancer – be fully removed if you previously told me *it* pierced through the wall of the colon? I could sense this conversation was going nowhere. It was as if I was asking the doctor his favorite color and he responded "kitty cat". He offered a possible solution: surgery. No, thanks. In case you haven't noticed she is too frail and will probably die on the operating room table.

A few days before we left for Kristen's wedding in Baltimore, Maryland, Mom's care coordinator called to inform me her hemoglobin was extremely low and sought my permission to have her transported to a local hospital for a blood transfusion. I agreed. I have always battled anemia, genetically this condition must have passed from Mom to me.

The next day she was brought to *her* hospital, Memorial Hospital, as Kathy and I were in another part of the state picking up last minute items to bring with us to the wedding. My cell phone rang and a doctor from *Mom's* hospital said Mom was refusing the transfusion. I told her to tell Mom that not having the transfusion is not her choice and that I was the one who ordered it.

We made it to the hospital in about forty-five minutes. When we walked in Mom's room, the doctor who called me and a nurse were chatting with Mom. As soon as she saw me she said, "Oh, look. There's my husband." The doctor corrected her and said that I was her son. As the doctor was leaving she said it was not uncommon for a patient in Mom's condition to become disoriented. Disoriented? Doctor, you don't know the half of it.

Returning from the wedding, we visited Mom back at the nursing center. Although it was still daylight outside, her window drapes were drawn and other than the light coming from the television, the room was in total darkness. Mom was sleeping when we walked in. A few minutes passed and I told Kathy we should leave without disturbing her. As we left the room, Kathy stopped and looked at one of the many pieces of paper taped to the door which was wide open, against the darkened room's wall.

One of the posted pages stated that before entering Mom's room to check with one of the nurses.

We stopped at the desk to find out what was going on and we were told that Mom had contracted a contagious MRSA infection while receiving her blood transfusion. Kathy asked if that was the reason there was a surgical mask in the trash basket in her room. The nurse said everyone entering Mom's room must wear a mask.

Great. We had just been in the room. Neither of us wore masks because who could read a maroon piece of paper with a black text message on a door flush against the wall of a blackened room?

The following morning I called Mom's nursing coordinator to tell her of our experience. She was extremely apologetic, especially knowing of my health issues, and told me Mom was being treated with antibiotics. A series of three tests would be administered over the next weeks to verify the MRSA was out of her system.

Our next visits were brief and, you can be assured, we wore masks.

One morning Mom called me to ask what I told Claire. I told her the only Claire I knew in the area was our realtor friend Claire. No not your Claire, she corrected me, *my* Claire. She said Claire was the friend who would drive her to play cards. Then it clicked, oh, that Claire.

"I've never spoken to your friend."

"Yes you did, I'm all packed and she was supposed to be here first thing this morning to pick me up and bring me home. You told her not to come." Mom was bedridden, how could she pack or go anywhere? She seemed satisfied when I told her I would contact her Claire and tell her Mom was waiting for her.

As the days passed, there was a physical change in Mom. She would want to spend most of her day sleeping. The staff did their best to dress her and get her up for all of her meals but her appetite had diminished. Even as I encouraged her to eat to regain her strength in order to move into the assisted living apartments in the next building, she would nibble but not really eat.

It was an effort for her to speak. When she did it was in slow, almost inaudible short sentences. Oftentimes she would stare at Kathy and say "Kathy" and then stop. Kathy would respond, "Yes, Mom." Then nothing, she would not make an effort to continue her thought.

I received a call from Mom's coordinator recommending Mom be moved to their skilled nursing floor where she would be able to receive more specialized care. I was in complete agreement. She also recommended hospice get involved, not necessarily because Mom was facing immediate death, but more for their expertise at pain management, as well as other related hospice services. I agreed to this as well.

Visiting Mom on the new floor we found it to be a much more tranquil environment. The nursing staff continuously flowed in and out of her room. Despite the extra attention Mom no longer spoke, remained in bed and her already poor appetite worsened. She would stare when spoken to and then trail off to sleep. I made a video of some of the pictures taken at Kristen's wedding. I kept it short; it was about a minute and a half, because I knew her attention span was reduced. As I played it for her on my laptop, she fell asleep.

As we were leaving, Kathy returned to Mom's room and changed the channel on her television. In the event Mom would awaken she would see her beloved Red Sox as they played in the World Series.

Later during that last week in October, our Thursday night visit was exactly the same as all of the other recent visits. We went into Mom's darkened room and attempted to communicate our presence before we left. Stopping at the nurses' station for any updates, the nurse paged through Mom's records and said Mom had eaten all of her lunch that day. I thought it was strange, since Mom had been refusing to eat for a little over a week, and over the past few days was refusing liquids as well.

Eating a full meal? Was her body rebooting itself?

17. It's Not Over Until Miss Lynn Says It's Over

At 9:08AM on Friday my cell phone rang. The caller ID indicated it was from Charlesgate Nursing Center. Kim, my mom's hospice nurse, was calling to tell me to get to the nursing home quickly, as Mom's latest blood oxygen level was down to 70%.

For those who are not aware, measuring blood oxygen level is accomplished with a finger tip blood oxygen monitor. A normal blood oxygen (blood ox) level ranges from 95% – 100%. Levels going down to 90-92% are not all that uncommon and usually not alarming.

As it was explained to me, besides monitoring the vital signs of a dying patient, a declining blood ox level indicated the body was in the final stages of dying. When the various organs shut down, the body tends to have the heart pump more blood to the damaged/dying organ in an effort to revive the organ's functioning and away from the extremities (hands and feet). Less circulation to the fingers, for example, would indicate a re-routing of life essential blood. Thus the blood ox level drops in the extremities. Shortly, without blood flow the fingertips will become cold to the touch and start to turn bluish.

After Kim's call, I sent a text message to Kathy who was at school. Not receiving an immediate response, I called and left a voice mail message on her phone. Still not receiving a response, I brought my phone with me as I began shaving. Kathy called as I was getting into the shower and said someone would cover her classroom and she was heading home to pick me up.

Stepping into the shower, I recalled my conversation with Kim about Mom's death being imminent. I chuckled and thought, "You don't know my mother. No one tells her when it's her time to die. She will tell you when it's her time to die."

When we arrived at the nurse's station on Mom's floor, Kim from hospice introduced herself to us. Prior to that I had only spoken to her on the phone when she called to update me after each visit with Mom. She reiterated the morning's declining changes to Mom's body and how in spite of it all, Mom remained peaceful, although she had not spoken or communicated with us in any way for just over a week. Entering Mom's room we saw no visible change from when we left her the previous night. Her breathing remained shallow and she still did not open her eyes when we spoke to her.

Near noon she started to develop an occasional gurgling in her breathing. We were told this was caused by the accumulation of saliva in her throat, which interferes with the swallowing process. Kim assured us that Mom was not experiencing any discomfort despite the gurgling noise which we, like most people at the bedside of a dying person, found terrifying to listen to. We were then assured that they would be upping the medication used to dry up the excess secretion.

Mid-afternoon I was startled to see our son, Matthew, coming through the door. Having been a nationally recognized shot putter, you can understand how his frame could amply fill the door frame. Unbeknownst to me, Kathy had called him at his school (he's a physical education teacher) to be with me while Kathy, ever the teacher, went back to her school in order to pick-up students' papers to correct.

As he walked down the corridor leading to Mom's room, he heard the blasting televisions from other patients' rooms and said, "Dad, with your hearing, you'd be right at home here." I told him to watch out; hearing is the last sense to go. "In that case, I assume with your lousy hearing you're already well on your way out. How about we slap a toe tag on you and leave you here?" Kids at any age are overrated.

Later that night Mom's breathing seemed natural, the rattling had lessened and her vitals were approaching normal. Her blood ox level bounced back to the 90's indicating her blood was once again flowing to her fingertips, surprising everyone, mostly the nursing staff. When I was told her blood pressure was 124/72, I commented that it was much better than my own.

After hearing this news at around 10:30 PM, Kathy and I ran out to grab a gourmet meal at Dunkin Donuts: Bagel sandwiches, yum. While we ate our quasi meals back in Mom's room, we looked at the hospitality tray of coffee, pastry and muffins which Karen, the nurse in charge of the floor, had delivered to us earlier in the day. In addition to the greasy bagel sandwiches we had just consumed, we had put quite a dent in the baked goods since that morning. We laughed – our only laugh of the day – and wondered if it was humanly possible for anyone to have consumed more carbs than we had.

Saturday and Sunday the gurgling increased in intensity and frequency, and the grunting and groaning began. Although it was agony remaining in the room and witnessing this seemingly downward death spiral, it would have been even more tortuous not to be there.

The morphine had been increased to a dose every four hours from a dose every six hours. You could tell when it was wearing off because Mom's increasing discomfort was displayed in her labored breathing and rattling.

By Sunday night, Mom's vital signs were still strong, yet her blood ox level started to drop into the 80's. During the drive home, I finally came to terms that Miss Lynn was getting ready to call it over and predicted that we would probably be getting THE call during the night.

On Monday morning when we entered Mom's room, it was a scene of quiet serenity imbued with a deep sense of peacefulness. Her breathing was slow and steady and only a little labored. Occasionally her death rattle would increase in volume, but nothing compared to what we had listened to over the previous two days. Her blood ox level was holding in the 70s.

At one point while Kim was in the room, my mom, who had been lying with her arms by her side since we arrived on Friday morning, raised her left arm as though signaling whoever was approaching to keep away from her. I assumed she was seeing something we were not and was communicating to whomever that she would decide when to go and it certainly wasn't going to be at that particular moment. Defiant to the very end.

As the hospice nurse was concluding her visit, she went over to Mom, bent close to Mom's ear and said, "Lynn, it's Kim. Open your eyes, Lynn. Open your eyes, your son is here."

Amazingly Mom responded for the first time in over a week. She briefly opened her eyes and without moving her head looked at us. Kim encouraged me to lean down and once again tell Mom it was okay to let go. "Mom, I want you to know that I'm fine. Kathy's fine. And, the kids are fine. We love you. It's time for you to go, Mom, it's okay. Uncle Ernie will be joining you soon. [Her brother was also terminally ill.] You've got to get going so you can show him the ropes when he gets there."

In the hall, Kim spoke of Mom nearing her end, and told us to contact any relatives and friends who wanted to say good-bye to her. They would have to come to the nursing home as quickly as they could. She added that oftentimes the dying person will fight to not die in front of their family. This might be the case with Mom. We said our good-byes and went home.

Within hours of our departure, at 2:20AM, Bob from hospice called to inform me that Mom had died at around 2:15AM. I turned to Kathy and said, "Finally after 85 years, she's at peace, no more personal wars to wage. No more hate mail to write. And, she left on her terms when she was damn good and ready."

18. Immortality At Least Temporarily

In spite of his best efforts, man has yet to crack the code to immortality. That's man. That's not Miss Lynn.

Eight years ago, she followed through on her lifelong desire to donate her body to science by signing up for Brown University's Medical School to receive her donated cadaver upon her death. There is no doubt in my mind that besides the obvious altruistic motive of providing medical school students with an insight as to how the human body works by dissecting her anatomy, Mom had another agenda for making this decision.

The estimated length of time the medical school will have her body is for a maximum of three years, after which time the body and all its dissected parts will be cremated. While Miss Lynn may not have discovered permanent immortality, she has found a clever way to have her pugnacious physical presence reside here on earth for another three years. *At least.*

I did not go to the nursing home to view my mom's lifeless body after I received THE call. I didn't want to admit that the saga of Miss Lynn was over, her final chapter written. Instead, I can imagine her legend continuing at least for another three years, that dying thing was only a passing phase: "Everyone thought I died, but I showed them…"

19. Return to Mayberry

Mom died early Tuesday morning and her brother, Ernie, passed the following Monday night. Incredible. Sister and brother dying of unrelated diseases a few hours shy of a week of each other. On second thought, I guess it's not all that surprising: Uncle Ernie always did follow his sister's lead.

Uncle Ernie's children asked me to deliver his eulogy. During the funeral mass, my mind wandered, and I looked around the church at those who had come to uncle's last party to celebrate his life. Auntie Dina, Mom and Uncle Ernie's youngest sister, already beginning her walk on the Alzheimer's path, was there with her family. Their other sister, Dorothy, a long time Alzheimer's sufferer was not able to attend. I saw a good number of my cousins and thought about those cousins who had already passed on.

Delivering an upbeat, off-the-cuff, spontaneous eulogy (How could it be anything else? We're talking about jokester Uncle Ernie here) was easy given my firsthand knowledge of Uncle Ernie and his high jinks as an integral member of the *Kids Behaving Badly* team. While speaking I glimpsed the faces of my cousins and their families and wondered why I never was more a part of their lives or they of mine. Why my children would be unable to pick any of their cousins out of a lineup nor them mine.

Returning to St. Maria Gorretti's felt like coming full circle. I had left their elementary school at the beginning of 7th grade when we moved to Connecticut. The school, which adjoined the church, was no longer a parish school but a regional Catholic high school.

Nevertheless, standing at the front of the church, surrounded by family, I suddenly felt transported back to earlier years of safety and innocence, my own version of Andy Griffith's Mayberry.

The collation after the funeral was held at a local bar, a favorite haunt of Uncle Ernie's. Speaking with my cousins, I started to realize that it was not they who isolated themselves from me, but Mom who isolated me from them.

Years of Mom going on about what this cousin had said about me behind my back, or the way another cousin was horrified by the way Mom's only son and his wife treated her. Although I learned long ago to dismiss most of Mom's contrived statements supposedly coming from the mouths of others, hearing them so often did leave me feeling cautious. I thought if I stayed away from her family, I would not be hurt if, in fact, someone was talking badly about my wife or me based on Mom's fictitious accounting.

I wondered how much different our lives would have been had Mom not driven a wedge between my cousins and me. Since we were all around the same age and started having children around the same time, how different it would have been had my family been part of their large and loving extended family of aunts, uncles and cousins.

Leaving "Mayberry" and the "what ifs" of the past behind us, Kathy and I drove home. Little did we realize that we would be making the same drive again less than two months later for the wake of my cousin David Savastano, Mom and Uncle Ernie's nephew.

20. Of Course Miss Lynn Would Get the Last Word

Nine years ago when I was Facing emergency open heart bypass surgery, I stayed up most of the night before the scheduled operation writing letters to Kathy and each of our four children to be opened in the event of my death. I told each of them how much I loved them and how incomplete my life would have been without any one of them.

In May of that year, Kathy and I celebrated our twenty-sixth anniversary. I wanted her to know those twenty-six years of our love for each other would remain in my soul for all eternity. She taught me how to love and provided me with the stability and security I never knew existed. And a family life I'd never had.

To our oldest child, Kristen, I wrote that even though she had a strong independent side, her directness and ability to handle complex situations, regardless of the circumstances, would guide her in taking over leadership of the family helping them to remain united through this period and into the future.

To Matthew, our oldest son, I pointed out that although he might resemble Rambo on the outside, he also had a sensitive heart the size of Montana beating within. I added he would now have to step up to the plate and be the pulsating heartbeat of the family. To make sure the family is kept together and centered on their mom.

To Michael, our middle son, who is most like me when it comes to injustice, I urged him to continue to be sensitive to the needs of others, shout the loudest for those underdogs who have no voice regardless of the consequences. To keep venturing out of his comfort zone like his sister (and me), explore the unknown and adapt easily to change.

To our youngest son, Mark, who has a keen sense of humor with a sarcastic bent (I don't know where he gets it from, must be his mother), I wrote of his compassionate side, which will help him break through the strongest barriers in life. I added a request that he keep those one liners coming to entertain me on the other side.

My last words to each of them were to follow their passion in life, just as I had. It might not make you the wealthiest guy on the block but it will surely make you the happiest.

My mother also left me a letter to be opened upon her death as a lasting memory of her.

Written on the envelope:

"Upon my death please see to it that my son, Andrew, receives this. Thank you. Lynn."

Letter:

"May 26, 1978 – My son Andrew married Kathy R. I knew something was wrong that very day. I met Kathy in church before the service and began telling her how lovely she looked, and she did, but I sensed something was wrong because she looked at my outfit, turned her back to me and proceeded to talk to other guests around us. I found out later that she was angry because I was dressed in champagne rather than blue that she had requested.

I did not know this was the reason for her ugly treatment of me, however, my husband chose this outfit as he was dressed in a beige suit. We shopped for three weeks for a blue gown but they were not the type of gown I could enjoy so upon being shown the outfit in a very exclusive salon, my husband loving it, the gown was exact so we bought it.

I was later told by Kathy "my mom wanted to wear champagne but I wanted blue." So I began to understand what my life was going to be like here on. Well the wedding began and I was determined not to allow her to ruin the day.

The day was great. My husband paid for open bar so the guests had all the cocktails they wanted and were very happy.

Wedding over – Rusty and Kathy left for their honeymoon on a trip to Acapulco compliments of my husband and I.

They have now returned from their trip and began their life together in a rented apartment, third floor.

Kathy's mom told me the same story about a telephone call <u>must</u> be made to them before a visit as they had told me and so we lived by their wishes.

However, since this was their first winter in their new apartment they soon realized it was a very cold apartment but said nothing. My husband and I were invited to dinner, along with Kathy's parents and as we were dining we noticed the curtains on the windows were swaying due to the draft of the wind. It was very cold in the apartment and my husband and I knew we had to help them – this was in November – so.

We had a 26 room house, had already made an apartment on the second floor and rented it to a very nice couple. We discussed offering it to Kathy and Rusty. They happily accepted so we had the ugly task to tell the tenants of the situation. They were sad but agreed by August to leave.

Moving time – briefly – boxes upon boxes were carried down the two flights of stairs by no one other than me and my cousin Jill and then carried into the second floor new apartment. Well, Kathy was never satisfied. She already had bedroom one, living room with fireplace, bathroom, kitchen and a spare room to be used as a nursery room.

One year later, she informed me that she was pregnant and would have to leave our home – needing more room. At this time, I had just divorced my husband so I offered them my home which included first floor and second floor and I would retain the one bedroom on the first level and the kitchen combined with sitting room on the second level. Well I was "put out" on the second level as they took in a friend to live in the studio apartment so now I am living in one room. What next, (I ask myself).

Well, Xmas season arrived and I was to learn that Kathy invited the guests, (all employees of ours to a Xmas party – IN MY HOME and not inviting me.

At the time I was president of a very successful travel agency which they soon took over leaving me as an "employee". Bad? – not bad enough – as I was brought to court by my own son for using the company name as my own!

I did go to court and his attorney which I once had as my attorney, felt so bad of the situation, he put his arm around my waist (in the courtroom) and said, "Lynn, you don't deserve this and noticed I did not have an attorney." He said, "Where and who is your attorney." I smiled and said "My attorney (you) has been taken away from me so I am going to represent myself." He looked sad and said "I know you can handle this case, good luck." I felt sad for him because he did not want to hurt me. Well.

The judge called our names, case to be heard. When he heard it was son against mother, he held the case in his chambers.

I WON THE CASE.

Now more sad news to follow.

Kathy and Rusty told me on a Tuesday, they were moving out on the Friday and Saturday of same week.

Although Kathy in her usual manner left our home without much notice, I rented the apartment she had and all was well.

Now at this time I am faced with a large house, recently divorced and no income so reluctantly my house went up for sale. It was sold immediately and I left the state for Florida.

I was very happy in Florida and returned two years later believing my son when he said, "The children need a grandmother." Then I remembered the days when living in the same house, Kathy placed large cartons against the door leading into her apartment so I could not see the baby.

I drove home from Florida for ten days was invited to their "new home" one time.

The three children were beautiful and happy to see nana. I was not invited again.

left for Florida very sad. Never a telephone call from them. And I would call to ask if all is well.

Knowing at this point that being a part of their lives was useless, I returned to Florida and bought a condo on the waterfront. I was finally able to regain my senses then a call from Rusty asking me to return "home" to help the business which I did on the condition I would stay six months and return to Florida.

During this time, I worked in New Haven to improve the travel business in the agency no longer belonging to me·– paid my own gas expense, never received a paycheck. Never invited to their home. At this time they bought a four bedroom house they could not afford. Had four children and often asked me to "babysit."

I was shut out of the business and was asked to babysit. The former "sitter" got paid very well but became ill so I was asked to "fill in". Never got paid I finally told them I had to get paid something as I had no income and was maintaining an apartment. At this point I was coming for four children. I loved every minute being with them.

I was reprimanded for washing the kitchen floor and the windows so I decided I had to leave there before I had a breakdown.

I remember the time when Matthew was 5 years old and in the hospital. I was using crutches as I had a knee replaced. Rusty and his wife did not ask me about the purpose of using crutches. I hobbled in the hospital to see Matthew.

January 21, 2010 – Telephone message to me, don't have to call there, anymore.

I remember the day Kathy shouted at me, blaming me for washing Rusty's shirt with color clothes resulting in the color running into the white shirt. I did not use her washer so I ask – why was I blamed?

I later found out from Kathy's family that she was a constant liar and blamed all others for her wrongdoing.

In 1986 – I could not walk well as I had to have hip surgery. They invited me for a birthday lunch - - I was brought to a restaurant called Panera's in Smithfield for a bagel and coffee. Following lunch at Panera's I was rushed out of the restaurant, unable to walk without pain, as they almost ran ahead of me, leaving me to walk alone.

And in May of 1999 – I was invited to a birthday dinner and they didn't show at the restaurant leaving me alone. They later told me there were there looking for me. But guess what – the hostess had me seated at the first booth so they could not miss seeing me. We watched each patron coming in – they did not show –

Then well now the sad news that Rusty's father died. His new wife Val, sold their home and after moving to one condo and then another was asked by Kathy to come live with them.

This pleased me because Val was alone, I told Rusty to be kind and nice to her. I really liked Val. She made a good wife for my ex husband.

Well Val moved in to their home and at this writing is still there. A mutual friend told me she (Val) was not happy there.

I asked myself – what is wrong in that house. They have four adult children and none of them live at home. Does that make one wonder?

Well it is now January of 2010 and I was told not to call their house anymore.

So much more has happened but telling it makes me sick. So as of this date, January 21st, 2010 I will not call them anymore and I will keep the news abreast as it happens.

P.S. I called Rusty three times – <u>answering</u> his cell. This was his answer "Yeah, I'm returning your call, had two messages on the machine. Anyway. That's fine. Don't have to call here to find out what is going on. Everything is fine here." So my diary I will not call anymore.

January 24, 2010 – Rusty called and for the first time ever, I answered and then hung up. Perhaps now he will know how I felt for all the years he hung up on me. Well, he yelled at me the other day and told me not to call his home anymore. No good news to report.

December 24 – Rusty Kathy and three children arrived. I gave them gifts and they were gone within an hour. My new promise to myself. No more gifts. Just one for all. Andrew plus family give check with envelop to all receive no thanks at all.

December 28th – This is the end for this year 2010.

January 1, 2011 – We embark on another year. Hopefully it will change for the better for the world.

January 8 – My brother Al died. I called Rusty to inform him – he did not answer 'til the evening and told me he could not make the wake or funeral of his uncle. He was going to Florida with his family to select a house for his son as Michael was moving there to his new job. This could have been put off a day but I'm sure Kathy (wife) with her meanness would not do so. Again I'll say – "my poor son" – unable to do anything – eyesight "legally blind" places him in a position to do all that wife Kathy demands.

She has changed our lives so badly and completely.

January 8, 2011 – my brother Al died. I called Rusty's house. As usual, when my number appears on their phone they do not answer so I had a friend in Providence call she gave the message. This is what I got in response – phone rang, me "Hello". Rusty "Yeah. I got the message but we will not be around as we are leaving 2AM for Florida to help Michael find an apartment. End of that. His wife did not get on the phone to offer any comforting remarks of the death of my brother.

February 19, 2011 – rushed to hospital – could not breathe. In hospital 19th – 24th of February. Home one day rushed by rescue to hospital Miriam.

February 19th – 24th home one day – back to hospital Miriam 5 days. Rusty and Kathy visited one day only. Can't blame Rusty – he cannot drive due to his physical condition.

March 1 – Rusty and son came over for personal papers – guess he thought I was going to die – I did not.

Surprise – here I am – with the grace of God. It is now March 21st and still Rusty has not been over.

April 4th – finally Rusty called – informed me he and wife were leaving for Florida to visit Michael. They tell me they do not have any money yet flying to Maryland and Florida is nothing for them to go for 4 days. Hmmmmm – I live about 12 driving miles away but they cannot visit me!!!

Journal of hospital in February 2011 – Went to Memorial Hospital by rescue.

5 days – returned home.

Home 1 day – following day

Rescue brought me to Miriam Hospital 5 days. Rusty and Kathy came to visit at hospital one time – less than 20 minutes.

Upon my return from hospital Rusty and Matt came to visit. It lasted 20 minutes. That is the time allowed to visit his mother? Matt and Rusty came over – pickup the papers they took out of here – have not seen or heard from them since. Not even a telephone call from Rusty.

At this writing on March 22nd, I am still quite ill. Nurses just left – but I am trying to get well. I'm sure that death would have been happily accepted by Kathy. Stay away from her and family for the sake of Rusty. I don't want him to suffer for even talking to me.

Easter 2011 – Holy Thursday. You came over with Kathy. Then for the last time Kathy told me she was angry with me because I had a beige gown on and all others wore blue on her wedding day.

...

Mom went to her death believing her lifetime of baseless allegations and delusions; refusing to face reality, preferring to invent her own.

The only part of Mom's last venomous words I will comment on are the ones written about my Uncle Al's death. When Michael and I landed in Orlando, there was a voice mail message on my cell phone from Mom saying my Uncle Al had passed away. I called her to learn the details and told her we had just arrived in Orlando to find housing for Michael as he had only two weeks before starting his new engineering position there.

Mom gave me Auntie Joan's, Uncle Al's wife, telephone number, and I tried to call her to express my condolences. Not getting through, I called my mother back and asked her to tell Auntie Joan where I was and what I was doing. Mom said she would explain my situation to Auntie Joan.

Leaving the airport, we stopped at the first pharmacy we saw so I could pick-up a sympathy card. I wrote Auntie Joan a note expressing my sadness over Uncle Al's passing and why I was not able to be with her and her sons, my cousins, Tommy and David, during this sad time.

21. The End

The idea of writing a book about my mom has been simmering in me for years, for most of my adult life, actually. I decided to kick the book down the road until she passed. When she did, the book was waiting. "Miss Lynn" only took three weeks to write.

Some readers might be wondering why I'm throwing Miss Lynn under the Hartley Tours bus. The purpose of this book was not to get even with or trash Mom. I wrote it for me, and fortuitously it turned out to be exactly what I needed: Catharsis, understanding, and coming to terms.

In my early years, I'd watch the way my friends' and cousins' parents treated them and would wonder what was wrong with me. My parents weren't like that at all. Once in a while I'd hear an aunt tell a cousin, "Be home when the street lights go on. I love you." The "Be home" part was familiar. The "I love you part", not so much.

A few years before Mom died, I decided to add, "I love you" at the end of our phone calls. Initially silent, she eventually responded with an uncomfortable, mechanical and brisk, "I love you, too." I continued saying it, even when she didn't say it back, even when she'd hang up on me. Didn't matter.

Some people close to Kathy and me asked why I didn't just shut her out of my life once and for all. It's simple really. She was my mother. And I think somewhere along the line she also became my responsibility. I loved her, but any real emotional attachment I felt for her began to ebb the day she tried to upstage Kathy at her own wedding. It's a terrible thing to say, but in all honesty, by the time she died, I was there more out of a sense of duty than anything else.

There's a song from the Broadway musical (and movie) *A Chorus Line* entitled, "Nothing." Despite the drama student's best efforts, she was unable to feel any emotion until the end of the song, when she heard her drama coach died, she cried. Her tears weren't for her coach. Her tears were because she felt nothing.

When Bob from Gentiva Hospice called at 2:20AM to tell me Mom had died, I was relieved that finally her tortuous suffering was over. But beyond that, I felt nothing.

Okay, Another The End

For those of you interested in mental health, Miss Lynn never went to any kind of counseling. Her response when asked was, "I don't need counseling. It's you who needs counseling." Didn't matter who asked, me, her husbands, her boyfriends, friends: "I'm alright, the world's all wrong."

A friend, who read this book in its earliest stages, sent me an email and said besides having been delusional; your mom seemed to be suffering from a Narcissistic Personality Disorder (NPD). She said the textbook definition of people with NPD is they believe…

…the world revolves around them (the focus has to be on them at all times)

> *Whenever the festivity was held inside, almost on cue after the last guest had arrived, Miss Lynn would descend the grand front staircase to the spacious foyer below, dressed to the hilt and exemplifying the theme of the party. When the gatherings were held outside, the side staircase was substituted so that she could still make her entrance before descending to graciously greet the common folk waiting below. Invariably, she would be wearing a large tiara. Her Majesty, Miss Lynn, Queen of the Universe.*

…they fantasize about being successful (although in reality more than likely it's the opposite)

> *It didn't take very long before Mom said she was closing Simmons Tours because it had grown to be so successful she had no time for herself. Translation: No bus company (including mine), hotel, restaurant or popular attraction would work with Simmons Tours because of her high last minute cancel rate and/or non-payment.*

…they expect to be treated better than others (just because they feel they deserve it) but they in turn at times treat others arrogantly.

> *MISS LYNN: Do you know who I am?*
> *LYDIA (sweetly): No, dear, but I'm sure we'll find out and let you know by the end of the tour.*

MISS LYNN: I don't like your attitude. I'm Miss Lynn. I started this business years ago. And I have the power to never have you on any of my buses ever.

It makes sense. Everything she ever did (or didn't do) was rooted in one simple fact: She was incapable of feeling empathy by:

- demanding that a son in a tux leaving for his prom first go supermarket shopping for her or else he couldn't use *his* own car
- paying people with "Miss Lynn points" and changing the point values as she went along and they were strung along
- agreeing to ride Hartley tour buses to Atlantic City as a passenger just as long as she collected the tips given to the tour escort working the trip
- placing our hate mail in a neighbor's mailbox
- leaving despicable messages on an answering machine in an effort to inform grandchildren during their early school years just how bad their parents are

In looking back, she couldn't have been different even if she'd tried. I take some comfort from that.

Be at peace, Miss Lynn.

Dear Reader:

Thank you for allowing me to share Miss Lynn with you.

If you enjoyed the book and would like to contact me, you can shoot me a brief email at: andyacci@andyaccioli.com and I'll personally respond.

I'd really appreciate if you stopped back on the page where you purchased *Miss Lynn: My Delusional Mother* and rate my book plus add any comment if you feel so inclined.

All the best,

Andy

P.S. You can subscribe to receive a *private*, emailed notification of my future book releases, book promotions, giveaways, etc. Simply visit my website: **http://www.AndyAccioli.com** and go to the 'Subscribe" page for more info.

Andy Accioli's Other Writings

Books: Nonfiction
Miss Lynn: My Delusion Mother
Diabetes Can Kill You

Books: Fiction
Altered Identity (#1 Troy McCoy Novel)
Darn Juan (#2 Troy McCoy Novel)
Where's Mal? (#3 Troy McCoy Novel)

Plays:

10 Full-length Plays: Earth To Ellen, Candy Apples, Truth Pants, Life Don't Give You No Do Overs, Yola's 90th Birthday Party, Long Live The Dead Pope, Rebel In The Ranks, At Heaven's Door and Caught Off Guard

Printed in Great Britain
by Amazon